Effective Communication Skills

Master Active Listening and Nonverbal Cues With 5 Proven Strategies for Better Relationships and Career Growth

Arnold Wolf

© Copyright Arnold Wolf 2024 - All rights reserved.

The content of this book may not be reproduced, duplicated, or transmitted without direct written permission from the author or the publisher.

Under no circumstances will any blame or legal responsibility be held against the publisher or author for any damages, reparation, or monetary loss due to the information contained within this book. Either directly or indirectly. You are responsible for your own choices, actions, and results.

Legal Notice:

This book is copyright-protected and only for personal use. You cannot amend, distribute, sell, use, quote, or paraphrase any part of the content within this book without the consent of the author or publisher.

Disclaimer Notice:

Please note that the information in this document is for educational and entertainment purposes only. All efforts have been made to present accurate, up-to-date, reliable, and complete information. No warranties of any kind are declared or implied. Readers acknowledge that the author is not engaging in the rendering of legal, financial, medical, or professional advice. The content within this book has been derived from various sources. Please consult a licensed professional before attempting any techniques outlined in this book.

By reading this document, the reader agrees that the author is under no circumstances responsible for any losses, direct or indirect, incurred as a result of using the information contained within this document, including, but not limited to, errors, omissions, or inaccuracies.

Contents

Introduction   1

Chapter One   3

  Empathy as a Communication Tool
  Psychological Barriers to Effective Communication
  The Power of Active Listening
  Nonverbal Cues: Reading Between the Lines in Business Interactions
  Feedback Loops: Ensuring Your Message Is Received as Intended
  The Importance of Tone
  Emotional Intelligence:
  The Art of Questioning: Engaging Others to Open Up
  Building Rapport: The Foundation of Effective Business Negotiations

Chapter Two   31

  Simplifying Complex Ideas for Your Audience
  Storytelling in Business: How to Engage Your Listeners
  Persuasive Communication: The Structure of Influence
  The Role of Language in Shaping Your Business Image
  Avoiding Jargon: Making Your Message Accessible to All
  Elevator Pitches: Conveying Value in Seconds
  Communicating with Confidence: How to Overcome Public Speaking Anxiety
  Mastering Meetings: Facilitation and Participation Techniques

Chapter Three — 57
- The Psychology of Listening: Why It's Harder Than You Think
- Active Listening in Negotiations: The Key to Unlocking Value
- Listening for What's Not Said: Nonverbal Cues and Silent Signals
- Empathic Listening: The Path to Deeper Business Relationships
- Feedback: Giving and Receiving Constructively
- Listening Challenges in Digital Communication
- Overcoming Selective Hearing in High-Stakes Situations
- The Role of Silence in Effective Communication
- Cultivating Patience: A Virtue in Listening
- Transformative Listening: Changing Perspectives and Outcomes

Chapter Four — 85
- The Vocabulary of Body Language
- The Impact of Eye Contact on Trust and Persuasion
- Posture and Presence: Conveying Confidence Without Words
- The Subtleties of Spatial Dynamics in Communication
- Using Gestures to Enhance Your Message
- The Power of Touch in Nonverbal Business Communication
- Dress and Appearance: Silent Communicators of Professionalism
- Nonverbal Cues in Virtual Meetings: Navigating the New Normal
- Cross-Cultural Nonverbal Communication: Navigating Global Business

Chapter Five — 113
- Email Etiquette: Crafting Messages That Get Read
- Leveraging Social Media for Professional Communication
- Video Conferencing: Tips for Effective Virtual Meetings

Managing Digital Distractions: Maintaining Focus in a Connected World

The Art of Digital Listening: Engaging with Your Online Audience

Digital Body Language: Understanding the New Cues

Crafting Your Digital Persona: Consistency Across Platforms

The Future of Communication: Trends to Watch

You Are Awesome!   138

Conclusion   141

References   143

Introduction

In a bustling coffee shop, two entrepreneurs sit across from each other, their conversation a delicate dance of pitches and counteroffers. But amidst the clattering of cups and the hum of background chatter, vital nonverbal cues are lost, and words meant to convey confidence are received as arrogance. The deal, brimming with potential, unravels—not due to a lack of opportunity, but from a failure in communication. This scenario, all too common in the fast-paced world of business, serves as a poignant reminder of the profound impact that effective communication—or the lack thereof—can have on our professional and personal lives.

I am Arnold Wolf, a seasoned business owner with over a decade of experience. I have delved deep into the realms of communication and negotiation. Driven by a passion for these arts, I dedicated myself to studying the practices of top-performing communicators. The culmination of my research and insights has been distilled into an easily digestible book, aimed at empowering others with the secrets of effective communication and negotiation strategies. My journey into the depths of negotiation and active listening has revealed to me the universal truth that, regardless of culture or industry, successful outcomes are often predicated on the quality of our interactions. With a mission to demystify the complexities of communication, I have dedicated myself to making nuanced negotiation and active listening strategies accessible to entrepreneurs and small business owners.

"Effective Communication Skills: Master Active Listening and Nonverbal Cues With 5 Proven Strategies for Better Relationships and Career Growth" is born out of a deep-seated belief in the transformative power of refined communication skills. This book does not merely aim to improve your ability to converse or negotiate; it endeavours to revolutionize the way you connect with others—be it in the boardroom or at the dinner table. Through a careful blend of practical strategies, real-world examples, and actionable exercises, tailored specifically for the entrepreneurial context, this book sets the stage for profound personal and professional growth.

In today's competitive landscape, the ability to communicate effectively is not just an advantage; it is a necessity. Research consistently shows that superior communication skills can significantly enhance negotiation outcomes, improve team dynamics, and foster stronger customer relationships. Yet, despite its critical importance, many of us struggle to communicate with clarity and empathy.

Structured in five comprehensive parts, this book guides you through the foundational theories of communication before diving into practical, hands-on strategies designed to elevate your listening and nonverbal communication skills. Each section builds upon the last, creating a holistic journey toward becoming a more effective communicator.

I recall a pivotal moment early in my career when a misunderstanding during a negotiation taught me the indelible impact of active listening. This experience, though humbling, underscored the profound difference that nuanced communication can make—not just in securing a deal, but in building enduring relationships. It is these personal lessons and professional insights that I share with you in these pages.

By embracing the strategies outlined in this book, you stand to gain not just better business outcomes, but deeper personal connections and a fresh sense of assurance in your capacity to navigate the intricacies of human interaction.. I encourage you to engage actively with the exercises provided and to keep a journal of your reflections and progress. This is not just a book to be read; it is an invitation to transform.

As we embark on this journey together, I invite you to approach this book with an open mind and a readiness to challenge your existing perceptions and habits. The path to mastering effective communication is both a science and an art, requiring diligence, empathy, and, above all, practice. Join me in transforming not just the way we speak, but the way we listen, perceive, and connect. Together, let's unlock the full potential of our personal and professional relationships.

Chapter One

The Role of Empathy in Building Strong Business Relationships

In a bustling urban landscape, the success of any business venture is often predicated on the ability to foster strong, enduring relationships. Central to this is the ability to communicate effectively, a skill that goes beyond mere verbal exchanges to encompass a deep understanding and connection with others. At the heart of such connections lies empathy, an often underestimated yet powerful tool in the business world. This chapter delves into the multifaceted role of empathy in building robust business relationships, distinguishing it from sympathy, exploring its impact on leadership, and offering actionable strategies to develop empathetic skills.

Empathy as a Communication Tool

Empathy: 'the capacity to understand and share the feelings of another' is more than a soft skill—it's a transformative tool that, when wielded with precision, can redefine business interactions. Consider a negotiation scenario where tensions are high, and stakes are even higher. An empathetic approach, one that genuinely seeks to understand the concerns and motivations of the other party, can diffuse tension and foster a collaborative atmosphere. This does not imply agreement but an acknowledgment of the other's perspective, creating a foundation for more productive and supportive dialogue. It's a shift from viewing negotiations as zero-sum games to collaborative problem-solving sessions.

Empathy vs. Sympathy

While often used interchangeably, empathy and sympathy hold distinct places in the context of business communication. Sympathy involves feeling compassion for someone else's situation without necessarily understanding their emotional state. Empathy, by contrast, involves stepping into another's shoes, seeing the world through their eyes, and experiencing their emotions. In a business setting, empathy enables a deeper connection and understanding, fostering trust and openness. For instance, when a team member misses a deadline, empathy allows a leader to understand the underlying issues—be it personal challenges or workload—thereby facilitating a supportive response rather than a purely critical one.

Empathy in Leadership

Empathy in leadership transcends mere understanding; it acts as a catalyst for team cohesion, loyalty, and performance. An empathetic leader is attuned to the emotional undercurrents within their team, enabling them to address discontent, motivate, and inspire effectively. Such leaders recognize that acknowledging the team's feelings and perspectives not only validates their experiences but also empowers them, fostering a sense of belonging and commitment. The research underscores the correlation between empathetic leadership and organizational success, highlighting that teams led by empathetic leaders often exhibit higher satisfaction, innovation, and performance levels.

Developing Empathy Skills

Empathy, like any skill, can be honed and developed. The cornerstone of this progress lies in active listening, which entails a deliberate endeavour to not only hear the spoken words but also comprehend the entirety of the message conveyed.. This involves paying attention to the speaker's body language, tone of voice, and emotional cues, offering a holistic understanding of their perspective. Another strategy is perspective-taking, an intentional effort to adopt another's viewpoint. This can be practiced through role-reversal exercises or merely by asking oneself, "How would I feel in their situation?" Lastly, cultivating a curiosity about others without judgment encourages open-mindedness and fosters deeper connections, paving the way for genuine empathy.

In practice, these strategies manifest in everyday business interactions, from how a manager responds to a team member's setback to the approach taken in customer service situations. By implementing empathy, businesses not only enhance their internal dynamics but also strengthen their relationships with clients, partners, and stakeholders, setting a solid foundation for sustainable growth and success.

In conclusion, empathy stands as a pillar of effective communication, its significance magnified in the realm of business where relationships dictate success. Through understanding, sharing, and acting upon the feelings of others, business leaders and entrepreneurs can create environments where collaboration flourishes, loyalty deepens, and performance soars. As we continue, the exploration of empathy's role within the intricate dance of communication will reveal its power not just as a skill but as a transformative force in the professional world.

Psychological Barriers to Effective Communication

How to Recognize and Overcome Them

Effective communication, while pivotal for the growth and success of any business, often encounters invisible yet formidable obstacles. These barriers, rooted deeply in our psychological makeup, can distort messages and lead to misunderstandings, significantly impacting business relationships and outcomes. Knowing these barriers is the first step towards mitigating their effects and enhancing communication within professional settings.

Identification of barriers

Several psychological barriers impede effective communication, including:

- Biases: Preconceived notions about individuals or situations that can cloud judgment and interpretation.

- Prejudices: Irrational and unfounded opinions that lead to unjust treatment and skewed communication.

- Emotional states: Mood swings or intense emotions, such as anger or sadness, that can alter the way messages are conveyed or received.

- Stress and anxiety: High levels can hinder one's ability to process information and communicate effectively.

- Cultural differences: Misinterpretations arising from cultural misunderstandings can act as barriers to clear communication.

Recognizing these barriers in oneself and interactions with others is crucial for any business leader or entrepreneur aiming to foster a culture of clear and effective communication.

Impact on business relationships

The presence of psychological barriers can lead to a cascade of negative outcomes within a business environment. For instance, biases and prejudices can prevent the formation of diverse teams, limiting creativity and innovation. Emotional states and stress levels can lead to miscommunications, causing conflicts and strained relationships among team members. Similarly, cultural misunderstandings can alienate clients or partners from different backgrounds, potentially leading to lost opportunities.

Furthermore, these barriers can distort messages, leading to a disconnect between what is said and what is heard. This discrepancy can cause confusion, errors, and inefficiencies, ultimately affecting the bottom line and the overall health of the business.

Strategies for overcoming barriers

To navigate the maze of psychological barriers, several strategies can be employed:

- Self-awareness: Regular self-reflection can help individuals recognize their own biases, prejudices, and emotional triggers. Keeping a journal or seeking feedback from trusted colleagues can be helpful practices.

- Mindfulness and emotional regulation: Techniques such as mindfulness meditation can aid in managing emotions and stress, leading to clearer communication. Practicing emotional regulation techniques ensures that communications are not clouded by transient emotional states.

- Active listening: This involves complete focus on comprehending the message rather than merely hearing it passively. Active listening helps in understanding the speaker's perspective and reduces misunderstandings.

- Cultural competence: Developing an understanding and appreciation for different cultures can mitigate misunderstandings that arise from cultural differences. This might involve learning about different cultural norms and communication styles.

- Open dialogue: Encouraging open and honest communication within teams can help in addressing and overcoming psychological barriers. Fostering a sense of understanding and collaboration creates a safe space allowing team members to feel comfortable.

Case studies

Real-life examples offer valuable insights into how businesses can overcome psychological barriers to improve communication:

- A tech startup, recognizing the impact of biases and prejudices on team dynamics, initiated a series of workshops aimed at fostering diversity and inclusion. These workshops included activities designed to challenge stereotypes and encourage empathy. As a result, the team saw an improvement in collaboration and innovation, with diverse perspectives driving the development of more comprehensive solutions.

- In another instance, a multinational corporation faced challenges in managing a culturally diverse team. Misunderstandings arising from cultural differences led to conflicts and inefficiencies. By implementing cultural competence training for its leaders and team members, the corporation improved its internal communication and collaboration. The training included modules on cultural norms, communication styles, and conflict resolution strategies from a multicultural perspective. This not only enhanced team dynamics but also improved the company's ability to serve a global customer base.

- A case involving a high-stress work environment revealed the negative effects of stress and anxiety on communication. The constant pressure to meet deadlines led to frequent miscommunications and a tense atmosphere. Recognizing the issue, the company introduced stress management programs, including mindfulness sessions and flexible work arrangements. These initiatives helped in reducing stress levels, leading to clearer communication and a more harmonious work environment.

These examples underscore the importance of recognizing and addressing psychological barriers in fostering an environment of effective communication. They highlight that with the right strategies, businesses have the ability to transform potential challenges into opportunities for growth and development.

The Power of Active Listening

What It Really Means and Why It Matters

Active listening stands as a cornerstone of effective communication, shaping the way messages are received and understood within the business arena. At its core, active listening involves a conscious effort to hear not only the words another person is saying but, more importantly, to comprehend the complete message being conveyed. This skill is pivotal in all forms of business interactions, from daily team communications to high-stakes negotiations, as it ensures that all participants feel heard and valued, thereby fostering a more collaborative and productive environment.

Components of Active Listening

Active listening is composed of several key elements that work in harmony to ensure a deep level of understanding:

- Full Attention: Giving the speaker undivided attention implies putting aside distracting thoughts and focusing solely on the speaker's words, tone of voice, and body language. This level of focus signals respect for the speaker and a genuine interest in what they have to say.

- Withholding Judgment: This entails keeping an open mind and refraining from forming an opinion or interrupting the speaker. It allows for a more objective understanding of the message being conveyed.

- Reflective Feedback: Providing feedback that reflects what has been heard helps to confirm understanding. This can involve summarizing the speaker's points or asking clarifying questions to verify that the message has been accurately received.

- Empathy: Attempting to understand the speaker's perspective and emotions adds depth to the listening process. It involves acknowledging the speaker's feelings, even if one does not necessarily agree with their point of view.

Improving Active Listening Skills

Enhancing one's active listening skills requires deliberate practice and mindfulness. Several exercises can facilitate this development:

- Focused Listening: Practice focusing solely on the speaker during conversations, avoiding the temptation to plan responses while they are speaking. This can be practiced in less critical communications to build the skill for more significant conversations.

- Silent Summarization: After a conversation, take a moment to silently summarize the key points made by the speaker. This exercise enhances the ability to retain and comprehend information.

- Empathy Exercises: Engaging in role-reversal exercises where individuals express a viewpoint and then switch roles to argue the opposite can enhance empathy and understanding.

- Feedback Loop: Implement a feedback loop with colleagues or friends where after a conversation, each party shares what they understood. This practice reveals gaps in communication and areas for improvement.

Active Listening in Negotiation

In the context of negotiation, active listening can be a game-changer. By truly understanding the other party's perspective and needs, negotiators can identify common ground and explore mutually beneficial solutions. This approach shifts the dynamic from adversarial to cooperative, opening the door to innovative solutions that satisfy both parties.

For example, during a negotiation, one party might express concerns not just about price but also about long-term reliability and support. An active listener would pick up on these underlying concerns and could propose a solution that addresses them, such as a longer warranty period or a dedicated support team. This not only meets the immediate need but also builds trust and rapport, laying the foundation for a lasting business relationship.

Active listening in negotiation involves several specific practices:

- Paraphrasing: Repeating what the other party has said in one's own words confirms understanding and shows that their concerns are being taken seriously.

- Asking Open-Ended Questions: Questions that cannot be answered with a simple yes or no prompt deeper insight into the other party's perspective. This can uncover underlying issues that might not have been explicitly stated.

- Noting Nonverbal Cues: Paying attention to the speaker's body language and tone provides additional context to their words, offering clues to their true feelings and concerns.

- Summarizing Agreements and Disagreements: Regularly summarizing points of agreement and disagreement helps keep negotiations on track and ensures that both parties are working from the same understanding.

Incorporating active listening into negotiation strategies not only facilitates more effective communication but also promotes a more amicable and productive negotiation environment. It allows negotiators to move beyond surface-level issues, uncovering deeper concerns and opportunities for compromise. This not only increases the likelihood of reaching an agreement but also enhances the quality and sustainability of the agreement.

Active listening, therefore, is not merely a passive act but a dynamic process that actively shapes the course of business interactions. By giving full attention, withholding judgment, providing reflective feedback, and empathizing with the speaker, individuals can significantly improve their communication skills. This, in turn, leads to better relationships, more successful negotiations, and ultimately, greater business success. Through conscious practice and application, active listening can be developed and refined, becoming a powerful tool in the arsenal of effective communicators.

Nonverbal Cues: Reading Between the Lines in Business Interactions

In the realm of business, where every handshake, every nod, and every pause carries weight, understanding nonverbal cues becomes a critical asset. These cues, often silent and subtle, can affirm or contradict spoken words, offering a deeper insight into the true message and emotions being conveyed.

Types of Nonverbal Communication

Nonverbal communication encompasses a wide array of signals, each carrying its own set of meanings and implications in business contexts:

- Body Language: The stance, posture, or movements of an individual can communicate confidence, openness, defensiveness, or anxiety. For instance, crossed arms might suggest resistance, while leaning forward could indicate interest.

- Facial Expressions: Often involuntary and universally recognized, facial expressions can convey emotions ranging from happiness and surprise to anger and sadness. A genuine smile can build rapport, while a furrowed brow might signal confusion or disagreement.

- The tone of Voice: It's not just what is said, but how it's said. The pitch, pace, and volume of a voice can add emphasis, convey sincerity, or hint at frustration, even when the words themselves are neutral.

- Eye Contact: Maintaining eye contact signifies attention and respect, whereas avoidance can be perceived as disinterest or discomfort.

- Touch: The use of touch, though less common in some business settings, can convey a sense of warmth and agreement when used appropriately, such as a firm handshake or a light pat on the back.

- Space: The physical distance maintained during interactions, known as proxemics, can indicate levels of comfort and familiarity. Too much distance can seem cold and impersonal, while too little can be perceived as intrusive.

Interpreting Nonverbal Cues

Interpreting nonverbal cues accurately requires an understanding of the context and a keen observational skill. Misinterpretations can lead to misunderstandings or missed cues about the emotional state or intentions of the speaker. For instance, a person may not be disinterested during a meeting but rather, might be concentrating deeply on the information being presented. Observing combinations of nonverbal cues rather than isolated signals can provide a more accurate reading of the situation.

Regular practice in different settings can refine one's ability to interpret these cues. Participating in or observing business meetings, negotiations, and even informal gatherings while consciously noting nonverbal communication can enhance this skill. Reflecting on these observations later to analyze the context and the outcome of the interaction can further deepen understanding.

The Role of Culture in Nonverbal Communication

Cultural differences significantly affect the interpretation and use of nonverbal cues. What is considered respectful and attentive in one culture might be perceived as rude or intrusive in another. Take for example eye contact, in some cultures it is seen as a sign of honesty and confidence, while in others, it might be considered disrespectful or challenging.

Navigating these cultural nuances requires a level of cultural competence that can be developed through research, exposure, and open-mindedness. Learning about communication styles and different cultural norms is essential for global business operations. When unsure, adopting a stance of observation and mirroring the nonverbal cues of others can be a safe and respectful approach.

Enhancing Your Nonverbal Communication

Improving one's nonverbal communication skills can significantly impact the effectiveness of business interactions. Some strategies include:

- Conscious Practice: Becoming more aware of one's facial expressions, body language and tone of voice in daily interactions can help in making intentional adjustments to convey the desired message.

- Feedback: Seeking feedback from honest colleagues or mentors on one's nonverbal communication can uncover blind spots and areas for improvement.

- Role-Playing: Engaging in role-playing exercises that simulate business scenarios is an effective way to practice and refine nonverbal communication skills.

- Professional Development: Workshops and training sessions focused on nonverbal communication can provide valuable insights and techniques for improvement.

- Observation and Mimicry: Observing effective communicators and mimicking their nonverbal cues can help in adopting more impactful communication strategies.

Improving nonverbal communication skills not only enhances the clarity and effectiveness of one's message but also contributes to building stronger, more positive business relationships. It signals attentiveness, respect, and sincerity, fostering an environment of trust and collaboration. Moreover, as businesses increasingly operate on a global scale, the ability to navigate and adapt to different cultural norms of nonverbal communication becomes indispensable.

In business, every interaction is an opportunity to connect, influence, and build relationships. By paying attention to the unspoken messages conveyed through nonverbal cues, professionals can gain deeper insights into the dynamics of their interactions, empowering them to communicate with greater effectiveness and forge deeper, more significant connections. Whether it's through a firm handshake, maintaining appropriate eye contact, or modulating one's tone of voice, mastering the nuances of nonverbal communication is a skill that can significantly enhance one's presence and efficacy in the business world.

Feedback Loops: Ensuring Your Message Is Received as Intended

In the landscape of business communication, the establishment and maintenance of feedback loops stand as pivotal mechanisms for ensuring that the intended message resonates clearly with its audience. A feedback loop, in essence, is a system designed to return information about the outcome of a process or activity. Within the context of communication, this system allows the sender to gauge whether their message has been understood as intended and, if not, to make the necessary adjustments.

Understanding Feedback Loops

At its core, a feedback loop involves two key components: the delivery of a message and the reception of a response to that message. This response, or feedback, is crucial as it offers understanding into the efficiency of the communication. In a business setting, feedback loops can take various forms, from formal review sessions to casual conversations. Their significance cannot be overstated, as they foster an environment of continuous improvement and adaptation, ensuring that communication strategies remain effective and aligned with business goals.

Creating Effective Feedback Mechanisms

To harness the full potential of feedback loops, businesses must establish mechanisms that encourage open and honest feedback. Some strategies for creating these mechanisms include:

- Regular Check-Ins: Scheduled meetings between managers and their teams provide a structured opportunity for feedback on communication effectiveness. These sessions can focus on recent interactions, projects, or presentations, offering a forum for constructive criticism and praise alike.

- Open Forums: Company-wide meetings or digital platforms where employees can voice their opinions and feedback about various aspects of the business, including communication practices. These forums promote transparency and inclusivity, making every team member feel valued and heard.

- Anonymous Surveys: Tools that allow employees to provide feedback anonymously can uncover honest insights into communication effectiveness. These surveys can be particularly useful in identifying issues that employees may feel uncomfortable discussing openly.

- 360-Degree Feedback: A comprehensive feedback system that involves obtaining feedback from a variety of sources, including peers, subordinates, and superiors. This provides a well-rounded view of an individual's communication skills and areas for improvement.

Implementing these feedback mechanisms requires a commitment to acting on the feedback received. This commitment demonstrates a genuine desire to enhance communication and nurtures a culture of trust and continuous learning.

Interpreting Feedback Accurately

The value of feedback lies not just in its collection but in its accurate interpretation and the action taken in response. Interpreting feedback accurately involves several considerations:

- Contextual Understanding: Recognizing the context in which the feedback was given is crucial. Feedback may be influenced by external factors such as project deadlines, workplace stress, or personal circumstances.

- Objective Analysis: Separating the message from the messenger allows for an objective analysis of the feedback. Focus on the content of the feedback rather than personal feelings towards the individual providing it.

- Seeking Clarification: When feedback is unclear or seems contradictory, seeking clarification can help in understanding the underlying issues. Asking open-ended questions can encourage elaboration and provide further insights.

- Synthesizing Information: Collecting feedback from multiple sources and synthesizing the information can reveal patterns and common themes. This holistic view aids in identifying the most critical areas for improvement.

Taking these steps ensures that feedback is not only gathered but also interpreted in a way that facilitates meaningful changes to communication strategies.

Case Studies on Feedback Success

Real-world examples underscore the transformative power of effectively implemented feedback loops:

- A software development company introduced monthly feedback sessions where team members could discuss communication barriers experienced during projects. This initiative led to the identification of a recurring issue with unclear project briefs. In response, the company developed a new template for project briefs, significantly reducing misunderstandings and improving project outcomes.

- In another case, a marketing firm utilized 360-degree feedback to assess the communication skills of its leadership team. The feedback revealed a perception of disconnect between the leaders and the rest of the team. To address this, the firm implemented a mentorship program, pairing leaders with team members. This program not only improved communication but also strengthened relationships across the company.

- A retail chain struggling with low employee morale used anonymous surveys to gather feedback on internal communication. The feedback highlighted a lack of recognition for employee achievements. In response, the company launched a weekly recognition program, acknowledging the contributions of employees. This initiative led to an increase in employee satisfaction and engagement.

These examples demonstrate how feedback loops, when effectively implemented and acted upon, can lead to significant improvements in communication practices, enhancing both individual and organizational performance. By fostering an environment where feedback is routinely sought, accurately interpreted, and constructively used, businesses can ensure that their communication strategies remain dynamic, responsive, and aligned with their goals.

The Importance of Tone

How Your Voice Influences Perception

The subtleties of how something is said often carry more weight than the words themselves. The tone of voice—a potent instrument in the symphony of communication—can significantly alter the perceived meaning of a message. It possesses the unique capacity to transform neutral sentences into expressions of enthusiasm, skepticism, or even disapproval, without altering a single word. This dynamic component of verbal communication plays a pivotal role in shaping business relationships and influencing how messages are received and interpreted by others.

The Impact of Tone on Message Reception

Imagine two scenarios where a manager says, "Great job on the project," to an employee. In the first, the manager's tone is warm, enthusiastic, and genuine. In the second, the tone is flat and disinterested. Despite the words being identical, the message received by the employee in each scenario is vastly different. The first scenario likely leaves the employee feeling appreciated and motivated, while the second could breed confusion or doubt about the sincerity of the praise. This example underscores how tone not only conveys information but also emotion, significantly affecting the receiver's perception and response.

Adjusting Tone for Different Contexts

Navigating the professional landscape requires versatility in tone to match the diverse settings and audiences encountered. A tone that exudes confidence and decisiveness might be well-received in a boardroom presentation, yet could be perceived as overly assertive in a one-on-one feedback session. Similarly, a tone that is too casual might undermine the gravity of a serious discussion, just as an overly formal tone could stifle open dialogue in a brainstorming session. Recognizing and adapting one's tone to suit the context and audience is a skill that enhances the effectiveness of communication. It involves:

- Assessing the Environment: Gauging the formality of the setting and the expectations of the audience.

- Purpose of Communication: Aligning tone with the intent of the message, whether it's to inform, persuade, motivate, or console.

- Cultural Sensitivities: Being mindful of cultural differences that might influence how certain tones are perceived.

Exercises to Control Tone

Developing control over one's tone involves both awareness and practice. A few exercises that can help improve this aspect of verbal communication include:

- Recording and Playback: Recording oneself reading the same sentence with different emotions and then playing it back. This exercise helps in becoming more conscious of how variations in tone change the perceived message.

- Mirror Practice: Practicing speeches or conversations in front of a mirror, paying close attention to facial expressions and how they align with the intended tone.

- Feedback Loop: Engaging in conversations with a trusted peer or mentor and asking for immediate feedback on tone. This real-time critique can provide insights into unintended tones and how to adjust them.

- Emotion Replication: Trying to replicate the tone associated with a range of emotions using a neutral sentence. This helps in understanding the subtleties in tone that convey different feelings.

Analysing Tone in Business Communication

Real-life business scenarios offer rich insights into the impact of tone on communication outcomes. Consider a scenario where a CEO addresses their company during a period of significant change. The CEO's ability to employ a tone that is both reassuring and confident can play a crucial role in maintaining employee morale and engagement. Conversely, a tone that betrays anxiety or uncertainty, even if the words are meant to reassure, can have the opposite effect, breeding unease and resistance among the staff.

Another scenario involves customer service interactions, where tone can be the difference between a satisfied customer and a lost one. A customer service representative who uses a calm, empathetic tone when dealing with a frustrated customer can defuse the situation and foster a sense of understanding and care. This not only resolves the immediate issue but also builds customer loyalty.

These scenarios highlight how mastering the nuances of tone can significantly enhance one's ability to navigate complex business communications successfully. Whether it's leading a team through change, negotiating a deal, or handling customer complaints, the right tone can open doors, build bridges, and solidify relationships.

Emotional Intelligence:

The Hidden Driver of Influential Communication

In the tapestry of skills that underscore effective communication, emotional intelligence emerges as a vital thread, weaving together self-awareness, empathy, social skills, self-regulation, and motivation. More than just a buzzword, emotional intelligence represents a deeper understanding and management of one's emotions and the emotions of others, facilitating interactions that are not only clear but also resonant on a human level.

The Components of Emotional Intelligence

At its core, emotional intelligence encompasses five critical components:

- Self-awareness: Recognizing one's emotional states, strengths, and weaknesses. This awareness allows individuals to understand how their emotions can affect their thoughts and behavior, as well as the impact on others.

- Self-regulation: The ability to manage one's emotions and impulses, adapting to changing circumstances without becoming overwhelmed. This skill is crucial in maintaining professionalism in high-stress situations.

- Motivation: A drive that goes beyond external rewards such as money or status. It includes a passion for work, a commitment to the organization's goals, and a propensity for optimism even in the face of failure.

- Empathy: The capacity to understand and share the feelings of another, a cornerstone of effective communication. It enables the communicator to tailor messages in a way that resonates with the audience's emotional state.

- Social skills: Proficiency in managing relationships and networks, navigating social complexities, and inspiring and influencing others. This component is vital in leadership, negotiation, and team collaboration.

Emotional Intelligence in Leadership and Negotiation

In the realm of leadership, emotional intelligence acts as a catalyst for fostering a positive work environment, enhancing team collaboration, and driving productivity. Leaders equipped with high emotional intelligence can better gauge the morale of their team, address conflicts more effectively, and motivate employees toward achieving common goals. Their capacity to understand and manage emotions contributes to a leadership style that is not just respected but also inspiring.

Similarly, in negotiations, emotional intelligence proves invaluable. It allows negotiators to read the room, understand the underlying emotional currents, and adjust their approach accordingly. This dynamic adaptability can lead to more fruitful discussions and outcomes, as negotiators can more effectively address concerns, build rapport, and find mutually beneficial solutions.

Improving Emotional Intelligence

Enhancing one's emotional intelligence begins with a commitment to personal growth and a willingness to step outside one's comfort zone. Several practices can aid in this endeavour:

- Reflection: Regular reflection on one's reactions to various situations can increase self-awareness. Keeping a journal to note emotional responses and the triggers behind them can provide insights into patterns and areas for improvement.

- Feedback Seeking: Actively seeking feedback from colleagues and mentors about one's behaviour and its impact can offer an external perspective, highlighting blind spots in self-awareness and social skills.

- Empathy Exercises: Practicing putting oneself in others' shoes, especially in conflict or misunderstanding, can enhance empathy. This could involve imagining the other person's perspective or engaging in conversations to understand their feelings and motivations better.

- Mindfulness and Stress Management: Incorporating mindfulness practices and stress management techniques, such as deep breathing or meditation, can improve self-regulation, helping individuals remain calm and composed under pressure.

Case Studies

A tech company CEO credited his company's turnaround to his focus on developing emotional intelligence among his leadership team. After a series of workshops and coaching sessions, the leaders exhibited improved self-awareness and empathy, leading to more effective communication and a significant boost in employee engagement and retention.

In another instance, a sales manager struggled with high team turnover rates and low morale. By adopting a more emotionally intelligent approach, focusing on empathy and social skills, the manager was able to rebuild trust within the team, leading to increased sales performance and a dramatic reduction in turnover.

A negotiation consultant shared an anecdote where a deal was at a standstill due to mounting frustrations on both sides. By applying emotional intelligence, specifically empathy and self-regulation, the consultant managed to de-escalate the situation, refocus the discussion on common goals, and ultimately secure a deal beneficial to both parties.

These stories highlight the transformative impact that emotional intelligence can have on communication, leadership, and negotiation. By understanding and managing emotions, individuals can navigate the complexities of human interactions more effectively, leading to stronger relationships, better decisions, and more successful outcomes.

In today's fast-paced and often high-stress business environment, the ability to communicate with clarity, empathy, and emotional intelligence is more important than ever. As we explore the multifaceted aspects of effective communication, it becomes clear that emotional intelligence is not just a supplementary skill but a foundational one, underpinning our ability to connect, persuade, and lead with impact.

The Art of Questioning: Engaging Others to Open Up

In effective communication, the ability to ask the right questions at the right time is akin to possessing a key that unlocks deeper levels of dialogue and understanding. This skill, when refined, can transform interactions from mere exchanges of information to opportunities for genuine connection and insight. It is within this context that we explore the nuanced art of questioning, a tool that, when employed with precision, encourages openness, fosters rapport, and facilitates a richer understanding of the people we engage with in our professional lives.

Types of Questions and Their Uses

At the heart of skilful questioning lies the distinction between open-ended and closed-ended questions. Open-ended questions, characterized by their ability to elicit detailed responses, invite reflection and elaboration, making them invaluable in understanding motivations, thoughts, and feelings. "What was your thought process behind this strategy?" is an example that encourages a detailed response, offering a window into the speaker's reasoning and perspectives.

Conversely, closed-ended questions, which can be answered with a simple "yes" or "no," serve the purpose of gathering specific information or confirming details. "Did you meet the project deadline?" is a straightforward query that seeks a direct answer, useful in clarifying facts or concluding discussions.

The strategic use of these question types, often in combination, can enhance the dynamics of business communication, allowing for both breadth and depth in the conversations that shape our professional interactions.

Strategies for Effective Questioning

The effectiveness of questioning hinges not just on the type of questions asked but also on how they are posed. A few strategies to enhance the art of questioning include:

- Building on responses: Using the information provided in answers as a foundation for subsequent questions. This technique demonstrates active listening and encourages the speaker to delve deeper into the subject.

- Maintaining neutrality: Framing questions in a way that avoids implying judgment or leading the respondent in a particular direction. This fosters an open and safe environment for genuine dialogue.

- Encouraging exploration: Asking questions that prompt the

speaker to consider new perspectives or alternative solutions. "What other approaches might we consider?" invites creativity and problem-solving.

- Balancing specificity with openness: While open-ended questions encourage depth, incorporating specific questions can help clarify and refine the discussion, ensuring a comprehensive understanding of the topic at hand.

Avoiding Leading and Loaded Questions

The integrity of communication can be compromised by leading and loaded questions, which subtly (or not so subtly) suggest the answer within the question itself. Leading questions, such as "Don't you think we should adopt this approach?" presuppose a desired answer, potentially stifling honest dialogue and independent thought.

Loaded questions, on the other hand, contain assumptions that may put the respondent on the defensive. "Why have you always been resistant to change?" assumes a pattern of behaviour that the respondent may feel compelled to refute rather than engage in an open discussion.

To circumvent these pitfalls, focusing on crafting questions that are free of bias and presupposition is crucial. This approach not only ensures the authenticity of the responses but also maintains the respect and dignity of all parties involved.

Practicing Reflective Questioning

Reflective questioning, a technique that involves rephrasing or summarizing what the speaker has said and posing it as a question, serves multiple functions in enriching communication. It confirms understanding, demonstrates attentiveness, and often encourages the speaker to expand on their thoughts. "So, if I'm hearing you correctly, your main concern is with the implementation phase?" is an example of a reflective question that validates the speaker's message and invites further elaboration.

This method not only deepens the conversation but also strengthens the rapport between the individuals involved, as it underscores a genuine interest in and respect for the speaker's perspective.

EFFECTIVE COMMUNICATION SKILLS

The art of questioning, with its ability to open doors to deeper understanding and connection, plays a pivotal role in the landscape of effective communication. By mastering the types of questions, employing strategic questioning techniques, avoiding the pitfalls of leading and loaded questions, and practicing reflective questioning, professionals can elevate their interactions, uncovering layers of insight and fostering an environment of open, constructive dialogue. This skill, nuanced and powerful, is a testament to the profound impact that thoughtful, intentional communication can have in the business world, transforming transactions into meaningful exchanges that drive mutual growth and understanding.

Mindful Communication: Present, Aware, and Focused

In the fast-paced environment of modern business, the ability to maintain presence, attention, and intention in communication is not just beneficial—it's transformative. Mindful communication, rooted in the principles of mindfulness, brings a heightened level of awareness to interactions, enabling individuals to engage more deeply and effectively. This approach to communication is grounded in being fully present, paying close attention to the conversation, and communicating with a clear purpose or intention.

The Principles of Mindful Communication

Mindful communication is built on three foundational principles:

- Presence: This involves being fully engaged in the here and now, not distracted by past conversations or future concerns. It means giving the speaker undivided attention, a rarity in today's multitasking world.

- Attention: Beyond just being present, attention requires actively listening to the speaker, and noticing their words, tone, and nonverbal cues. It's about truly hearing what is being said, beyond just the surface level.

- Intention: Every communication carries with it an intention, whether to inform, persuade, console, or connect. Mindful communication involves being clear about one's intention from the outset, ensuring that the message is aligned with the desired outcome.

Benefits of Mindful Communication in Business

Implementing mindful communication within a business context can lead to numerous benefits, including:

- Clarity in Understanding: When both parties are fully present and attentive, messages are less likely to be misunderstood. This clarity can prevent costly errors and misunderstandings.

- Reduced Conflict: Many workplace conflicts arise from miscommunications or lack of understanding. Mindful communication fosters a deeper understanding and empathy, which can significantly reduce the occurrence of conflict.

- Enhanced Relationships: By showing genuine attention and intention in communication, relationships within the workplace can strengthen. Colleagues and clients alike feel valued and heard, fostering a positive work environment and stronger business partnerships.

Practices for Developing Mindful Communication

Developing the skills necessary for mindful communication involves intentional practice. Some effective methods include:

- Mindfulness Meditation: Regular mindfulness meditation can enhance one's ability to remain present and focused, benefits that directly translate to improved communication skills. Even a few minutes a day can make a noticeable difference.

- Active Listening Exercises: Engaging in exercises specifically designed to improve listening skills, such as repeating back what has been said or summarizing the speaker's main points, can reinforce the principles of attention and intention.

- Intention Setting: Before any significant communication, taking a moment to clarify one's intention can help align the forthcoming message with the desired outcome. This practice ensures that communications are purposeful and aligned with one's goals.

- Digital Detoxes: Periodically disconnecting from digital devices, especially during important conversations, can help cultivate the habit of being fully present. This practice reduces distractions and enhances one's ability to engage in mindful communication.

Applying Mindfulness in Challenging Situations

High-pressure or challenging business scenarios test the limits of mindful communication. However, it is in these situations that such an approach can be most beneficial. Strategies for maintaining mindfulness in difficult conversations include:

- Breath Focus: When tensions rise, focusing on one's breath can serve as an anchor, helping to maintain calmness and presence. This simple technique can prevent reactive responses and ensure that communication remains constructive.

- Empathic Response: In challenging situations, striving to understand the other person's perspective and responding with empathy can de-escalate potential conflicts. This approach encourages a more open and productive dialogue.

- Pause Before Responding: Incorporating a brief pause before responding allows for a moment of reflection, ensuring that the response is thoughtful and aligned with one's intentions. This pause can be critical in maintaining the clarity and purpose of the communication.

- Nonverbal Awareness: Being mindful of one's nonverbal cues, as well as those of the speaker, can provide insights into the emotional undercurrents of the conversation. Adjusting one's posture, facial expressions, and tone to convey openness and attentiveness can positively influence the direction of the interaction.

Incorporating mindful communication into daily business interactions requires practice and intention. However, the rewards—clearer understanding, reduced conflict, and stronger relationships—are well worth the effort. By staying present, paying attention, and communicating with clear intentions, individuals can navigate the complexities of workplace interactions with ease and effectiveness. This approach not only enhances individual performance but also contributes to a more harmonious and productive organizational culture.

Building Rapport: The Foundation of Effective Business Negotiations

In the nuanced dance of negotiation, the establishment of rapport acts as a critical precursor to successful outcomes. This foundational element fosters a climate of trust and openness, paving the way for more fruitful discussions and mutually beneficial agreements. Rapport is not just about making a positive first impression; it is about cultivating a genuine connection that can withstand the rigors of negotiation and lay the groundwork for long-term collaboration.

Techniques for Building Rapport

Creating this essential connection involves several key techniques, each contributing to a deeper sense of understanding and camaraderie between negotiating parties:

- Mirroring: This subtle yet powerful technique involves subtly matching the body language, speech patterns, and energy level of the other person. Mirroring can create a subconscious sense of affinity and alignment without the other party necessarily realizing why they feel more connected to you.

- Showing Genuine Interest: Taking the time to learn about the other party's background, interests, and concerns conveys that you value them not just as a negotiating counterpart but as a person. This can be as straightforward as asking thoughtful questions about their experiences or expressing curiosity about their company's history and values.

- Sharing Personal Stories: Revealing aspects of your own background and experiences can humanize the negotiation process. When done appropriately, sharing stories can break down barriers and foster a sense of mutual understanding and respect.

These techniques, when employed with sincerity and tact, can significantly enhance rapport, creating a more conducive atmosphere for negotiation. However, their effectiveness lies in their genuine application; insincerity can be easily detected and may backfire, damaging trust rather than building it.

Maintaining Rapport Over Time

Beyond the negotiation table, the challenge often lies in sustaining the rapport built during initial interactions. Long-term business relationships thrive on continued trust, mutual respect, and ongoing communication. Strategies for maintaining rapport include:

- Regular Check-ins: Scheduled meetings or informal catch-ups can keep the lines of communication open, providing opportunities to address any issues and celebrate successes together. These interactions reinforce the sense of partnership and shared goals.

- Consistency in Words and Actions: Ensuring that your actions align with your words is crucial in maintaining trust. Consistency in follow-through on promises and commitments solidifies the foundation of rapport built during negotiations.

- Adaptability: Being receptive to feedback and willing to adapt strategies or approaches as circumstances change demonstrates a commitment to the relationship beyond the initial agreement. This flexibility can reinforce the bond between parties, showing that the relationship is valued even when adjustments are needed.

- Celebrating Milestones: Acknowledging and celebrating milestones or achievements in the partnership can strengthen rapport. Whether it's a successful project completion or the anniversary of the partnership, these moments offer a chance to reflect on the journey together and anticipate future collaborations.

Rapport-Building Challenges and Solutions

Despite best efforts, building and maintaining rapport can encounter obstacles, from miscommunications to changes in personnel.

Addressing these challenges requires a proactive and thoughtful approach:

- Miscommunications: Even with strong rapport, misunderstandings can occur. When they do, addressing them promptly and openly can prevent them from escalating. Seeking clarification and expressing your perspective calmly can help resolve conflicts and reinforce trust.

- Changes in Personnel: Business relationships often involve multiple individuals and changes in key personnel can disrupt rapport. When new members join the team, integrating them into the established relationship through introductions and shared experiences can smooth the transition and preserve the rapport.

- Cultural Differences: In global business settings, cultural differences can pose challenges to building rapport. Educating oneself about the other party's cultural norms and demonstrating respect for those differences can mitigate potential misunderstandings and foster a more inclusive atmosphere.

- Distance and Time: Remote negotiations or partnerships across time zones can make it more challenging to build and maintain rapport. Leveraging technology for video calls rather than relying solely on emails or phone calls can help maintain personal connection. Scheduling meetings at times that are convenient for both parties, even if it means making accommodations, shows respect for the relationship.

In building rapport, the goal is not to manipulate or to win at any cost but to establish a genuine connection that can lead to mutually beneficial outcomes. This foundation of trust and understanding not only enhances the negotiation process but also contributes to the sustainability and growth of business relationships over time. Whether navigating the initial stages of a negotiation or seeking to maintain a long-standing partnership, the principles of rapport-building serve as a guide to more effective and rewarding business interactions.

Chapter Two

Crafting Your Message for Clarity and Impact

In a world awash with information, clarity becomes the beacon that guides your audience through the fog. The hallmark of effective communication is not the complexity of your vocabulary, but the simplicity and purity of the message conveyed. Imagine explaining the intricacies of blockchain technology to a ten-year-old or demystifying the principles of quantum physics for a non-scientific audience. The challenge, and indeed the skill, lies in distilling complex ideas into digestible, relatable nuggets of wisdom. This chapter focuses on simplifying complex ideas, a critical skill that can make or break your communication efforts.

Simplifying Complex Ideas for Your Audience

Breaking down complexity

Complex concepts often intimidate and lose the audience's interest. The key to maintaining their engagement is breaking down these concepts into smaller, manageable parts. Start by identifying the core idea you wish to communicate. Then, deconstruct this core idea into its basic components, much like disassembling a machine to understand its workings. For instance, if you're explaining a complex business model, start with its goal, then discuss the key strategies, followed by the roles of different parts of the organization in implementing these strategies.

- Use real-life scenarios: Illustrate each component with a scenario your audience can relate to.

- Sequential explanation: Present the components in a logical sequence, building up the concept piece by piece.

Use of analogies and metaphors

Analogies and metaphors shine light on unfamiliar concepts by comparing them to familiar experiences. This technique bridges the gap between the known and the unknown, making abstract ideas more concrete.

- Select relatable analogies: Choose analogies that resonate with your audience's experiences or interests.
- Metaphors for visualization: Use metaphors that evoke vivid images, helping the audience visualize complex ideas.

For instance, likening a company's organizational structure to a beehive immediately conveys an image of bustling activity, hierarchy, and collective effort toward a common goal.

The importance of clarity

Clarity in communication ensures that your message is not lost in translation. It involves choosing your words for precision and understanding, structuring your sentences for easy follow-through, and consciously avoiding ambiguity.

- Prioritize key points: Highlight the most important information you want your audience to remember.
- Avoid jargon: Use simple language that your audience can easily understand.
- Short sentences: Keep your sentences short and to the point to maintain the audience's focus.

Clarity is not about dumbing down your message but about ensuring it is understood as intended.

Feedback for simplicity

Feedback is the compass that guides your efforts toward simplicity. It helps you gauge whether your message is hitting the mark or getting lost in complexity.

- Seek diverse opinions: Ask people from different backgrounds to review your explanation of complex ideas.

- Use questionnaires or surveys: After presenting a complex concept, use these tools to assess understanding.

- Adjust based on feedback: Use the insights gained to refine your message, simplifying further where needed or clarifying any confusing parts.

For example, after presenting a new software tool to a team, ask them to summarize the tool's purpose and function in their own words. Their responses will highlight areas that need further simplification.

By embracing these strategies, you transform dense forests of complexity into open fields of understanding, inviting your audience to journey with you to the heart of your message. Simplifying complex ideas not only demonstrates your mastery of the subject but also your commitment to effective communication.

Storytelling in Business: How to Engage Your Listeners

The narrative has always been a powerful method to engage and connect with others. In the business world, where facts and data often dominate discussions, storytelling emerges as a vital tool to breathe life into presentations, marketing efforts, and leadership practices. It's not merely about entertaining; it's about making your message resonate on a deeper emotional level, ensuring it's remembered long after the conversation ends.

The Power of Narrative

A well-crafted story can capture attention in a way no list of bullet points ever could. It transforms passive listeners into active participants, drawing them into a shared experience. Stories evoke emotions, making the message more impactful and memorable. When listeners are emotionally invested, they're more likely to remember and act upon what they've heard. This emotional connection is particularly crucial in today's information-saturated environment, where attention is the most scarce resource.

- Emotional resonance: Stories can stir emotions, whether it's inspiration, empathy, or even amusement, creating a lasting impression.

- Memory enhancement: Emotional engagement helps cement the message in the listener's memory, making it more likely to be recalled later.

- Engagement: A narrative pulls listeners into the story, engaging them fully and making them more receptive to the message.

Structuring a Compelling Story

Every memorable story follows a structure that guides the listener through a journey. This structure can be adapted to fit business contexts, whether you're crafting a brand narrative, presenting a case study, or sharing a vision for the future.

- Setting: Establish the context of your story. In business, this might be the market landscape before the introduction of your product or the challenges your team faced at the project's outset.

- Conflict: Introduce the problem or challenge. This could be an unmet market need, a significant hurdle your team had to overcome, or a personal obstacle on the path to leadership.

- Resolution: Share how the conflict was resolved. This is where you highlight the effectiveness of your product, the innovative solution your team developed, or the growth that resulted from overcoming personal challenges.

Crafting a narrative with these elements ensures your message is not only heard but also felt and remembered.

Real-world Applications

Incorporating storytelling into various business practices can significantly enhance communication effectiveness. Here are some areas where narratives can be particularly powerful:

- Presentations: Transform your presentations by weaving in

stories that illustrate key points. This could be a customer success story that exemplifies the impact of your product or a personal anecdote that underscores a leadership lesson.

- Marketing: Use storytelling to create compelling brand narratives. Share the story of your company's founding, the challenges it has overcome, and the difference it makes in customers' lives.

- Leadership: The use of storytelling is used to inspire and motivate their teams. Share stories of past successes, failures, and lessons learned to reinforce company values and vision.

Developing Your Storytelling Skills

Enhancing your ability to tell engaging stories requires practice and a willingness to observe and learn. Here are some exercises to refine your storytelling skills:

- Observation and note-taking: Pay attention to the stories that capture your interest in your daily life. Note what makes them compelling and consider how you can apply these elements to your storytelling.

- Creative thinking exercises: Challenge yourself to find the story in everyday situations. This could be imagining the backstory of a stranger you see on your commute or crafting a narrative around a new product idea.

- Practice and feedback: Share your stories with trusted friends or colleagues and ask for honest feedback. Focus on improving the clarity, emotional resonance, and engagement of your narratives.

The ability to tell a captivating story is not just a skill but a powerful tool that can transform the way you communicate in business. It allows you to connect with your audience on a deeper level, making your message more impactful and memorable. Whether you're presenting to stakeholders, marketing a new product, or leading a team, storytelling offers a path to more effective and resonant communication.

Persuasive Communication: The Structure of Influence

In the vast arena of business, where decisions teeter on the edge of words and perceptions, the power of persuasion emerges as a pivotal force. Persuasive communication transcends the mere exchange of information, weaving a narrative that influences, motivates, and ultimately shapes the decision-making process. At its core, persuasive communication harnesses the subtle art of influence, melding logic with emotion to guide audiences toward a desired conclusion. This section explores the foundational principles of persuasion, the craft of composing influential messages, the importance of ethical persuasion, and real-life instances of successful persuasive strategies in the business domain.

Principles of Persuasion

The science of persuasion rests on several key principles, each serving as a lever to influence human behaviour and decision-making. Understanding and applying these principles elevates the effectiveness of communication, transforming passive listeners into active participants.

- Reciprocity: The innate human instinct to return favours. In communication, offering valuable information or insights can prompt your audience to reciprocate in kind, enhancing engagement and openness to your message.

- Scarcity: Highlighting the uniqueness and limited availability of an opportunity can create a sense of urgency, making the proposition more attractive.

- Authority: Establish credibility and demonstrate expertise on the subject matter. Audiences are more inclined to be persuaded by sources that exude confidence and authority.

- Commitment: Encouraging small initial commitments can lead to more significant engagements over time, as people strive for consistency in their beliefs and actions.

- Liking: People are more persuaded by individuals they like or with whom they share similarities. Building rapport and demonstrating empathy can make your message more persuasive.

Crafting Persuasive Messages

The art of crafting persuasive messages involves a delicate balance between appealing to logic and emotion. The following techniques can enhance the persuasive power of your communication:

- Strategic storytelling: Incorporating stories that resonate with the audience's experiences or aspirations can emotionally invest them in your message, making it more compelling.

- Emphasizing benefits: Focusing on how your proposal benefits the audience personalizes your message, making it more relevant and persuasive.

- Contrasting scenarios: Illustrating the outcomes of taking action versus inaction can highlight the value and urgency of your proposition.

- Inclusive language: Using language that includes the audience in your vision or proposal fosters a sense of unity and shared purpose, enhancing persuasion.

Ethical Persuasion

In wielding the power of persuasion, ethical considerations must anchor your strategies. Ethical persuasion is grounded in honesty, transparency, and respect for the audience's autonomy. This ethical framework ensures that persuasive efforts bolster trust and credibility, rather than eroding them.

- Transparency: Being open about your intentions and avoiding manipulation. This includes clearly stating any potential biases or vested interests.

- Respect for autonomy: Ensuring that the audience feels free to make their own decisions without undue pressure or coercion.

- Accuracy: Committing to the truthfulness and accuracy of the information presented. Misleading or deceptive practices can have long-term detrimental effects on relationships and reputations.

Persuasion in Action

Analysing examples of successful persuasion illuminates the practical application of these principles and techniques:

A technology startup seeking investor funding utilized the principle of scarcity by emphasizing the unique, groundbreaking nature of its product and the time-sensitive opportunity for investors to get involved. Coupled with compelling storytelling that painted a vivid picture of the product's potential impact, the startup successfully secured the necessary funding.

In a campaign to enhance employee wellness, a corporation leveraged the principle of commitment by introducing a step-count challenge. Participants committed to a modest daily goal, which gradually increased. The challenge was communicated through persuasive messaging that highlighted personal and community health benefits, saw high participation rates, and significantly improved overall employee wellness.

A non-profit organization aiming to increase donations crafted a persuasive message centred around storytelling. They shared powerful, personal stories of those impacted by their work, effectively using emotional appeals to connect with potential donors. By demonstrating authority through data on their accomplishments and transparency about the use of funds, the organization saw a substantial increase in contributions.

These examples underscore the effectiveness of well-crafted persuasive communication in achieving business objectives. Whether securing investments, motivating teams, or driving social impact, the strategic application of persuasion principles can influence outcomes and inspire action.

The Role of Language in Shaping Your Business Image

The fabric of your business's identity is woven with the threads of language. Every word chosen and every style adopted sends a message to the world about who you are as a business and what you stand for.

EFFECTIVE COMMUNICATION SKILLS

This realization brings to light the profound influence of language on your business's perception by clients, partners, and even competitors.

Language and Perception

The decision-making process in selecting the right words and language style is akin to choosing the attire for a crucial business meeting. Just as the right outfit can instill confidence and command respect, the appropriate use of language can elevate your business's image, making it appear more professional, innovative, or approachable, depending on your strategic choice. For instance, a tech startup aiming to appear cutting-edge might incorporate the latest industry buzzwords into its communication, whereas a family-run cafe might opt for warm, inviting language to draw in customers.

- Precision and warmth: Balance these qualities in your language to tailor your business's perceived image.

- Adaptability: Be ready to evolve your language use in response to changes in societal norms or industry trends.

Consistency in Communication

The cornerstone of a reliable brand image is consistency across all platforms and mediums of communication. This consistency extends beyond visual branding elements to include the language and tone used in emails, social media posts, advertising, and even internal communications. It ensures that customers receive a unified message about what your business represents, regardless of where or how they interact with your brand.

- Brand style guides: Develop comprehensive guides that detail your brand's preferred language style, tone, and even phrases to use or avoid.

- Regular reviews: Periodically revisit and, if necessary, revise your language guidelines to ensure they remain aligned with your brand's evolving identity and values.

Adjusting Language for Different Audiences

While consistency is crucial, flexibility allows your message to resonate more deeply with diverse audiences. Tailoring your language to suit different segments of your audience—without sacrificing your brand's core identity—is an art that can significantly enhance the effectiveness of your communication.

- Market research: Understand the language preferences and sensitivities of your different audience segments.

- Customization: Adjust your language on platforms or materials targeting specific segments, ensuring it aligns with their expectations and preferences.

For example, communication aimed at a younger demographic might adopt a more casual, conversational style, while proposals for corporate partners maintain a level of formality and professionalism.

Language as a Tool for Inclusivity

In today's globalized world, inclusivity in language is not just a moral imperative but a strategic business decision. Inclusive language ensures that no potential customer or client feels alienated because of how communication is phrased. It reflects a business's commitment to diversity and equality, enhancing its reputation and broadening its appeal.

- Gender-neutral language: Use terms like "they" instead of "he/she" and job titles like "salesperson" instead of "salesman" or "saleswoman."

- Cultural sensitivity: Be mindful of phrases or references that may be offensive or exclusionary to people from different cultural backgrounds.

- Accessibility: Consider how your language might be interpreted by people with different abilities or those using assistive technologies.

Adopting inclusive language is not a one-time task but an ongoing process of learning, listening, and adjusting based on feedback and broader societal changes.

In the landscape of business, the power of language extends far beyond mere communication. It shapes perceptions, builds identity, and fosters relationships. Through mindful selection and use of language, businesses can craft an image that resonates with their values and aspirations, drawing customers closer and setting the foundation for lasting success.

Avoiding Jargon: Making Your Message Accessible to All

In the intricate web of business communication, jargon stands as a formidable gatekeeper, decipherable only by those within a specific industry sphere. While it may serve as shorthand among experts, its use can create barriers, obscuring the essence of your message from a wider audience. This section aims to shed light on identifying jargon, understanding its impact, and adopting strategies to ensure your communication remains clear and accessible, all while maintaining a balance between simplicity and demonstrating expertise.

Identifying Jargon

The first step toward making your message universally understandable is to recognize jargon. These are terms, phrases, or acronyms that hold specific meanings within a particular field but might be unfamiliar to outsiders. For instance, terms like 'SEO' (Search Engine Optimization) or 'KPI' (Key Performance Indicator) are commonplace in marketing and business analytics but can be perplexing to those not versed in these domains.

- Audit your communication: Regularly review your written and verbal communication to spot industry-specific terms.

- Seek outside perspectives: Ask individuals outside your field to identify terms in your communication that are unclear to them.

- Maintain a jargon glossary: Keep a list of identified jargon and their simpler explanations as a reference for creating future content.

The Impact of Jargon on Communication

Jargon can alienate or confuse audiences, creating a disconnect between your message and its reception. When listeners or readers encounter unfamiliar terms, they may feel excluded, leading to a loss of interest or engagement. Moreover, overuse of jargon can inadvertently signal a lack of consideration for the audience's background or knowledge level, potentially undermining trust and credibility.

- Audience alienation: When people feel excluded by the language used, they are less likely to engage with the content.

- Misinterpretation: Jargon can lead to misunderstandings, as people might misinterpret the term or miss the message entirely.

- The barrier to engagement: Complicated language can deter audiences from interacting with your message, whether it's a product, service, or idea you're trying to convey.

Techniques for Simplifying Language

Simplifying language without diluting the message's integrity or professionalism is a delicate balance. Effective communication should be clear and accessible, inviting engagement from a broad audience.

- Use plain language: Opt for words that are widely understood. Replace 'utilize' with 'use', 'facilitate' with 'help', or 'terminate' with 'end'.

- Explain as you go: When industry terms are unavoidable, follow them with a brief, simple explanation or analogy.

- Short sentences: Aim for brevity and clarity in sentence structure to enhance understanding.

- Active voice: Makes your writing clearer and more direct. For example, 'The team achieved the targets' instead of 'The targets were achieved by the team'.

Balancing Simplicity with Expertise

The ultimate goal is to communicate effectively, ensuring your message is both accessible and authoritative. Striking this balance demands a nuanced approach, respecting the intelligence of your audience while also guiding them through complex ideas with clarity.

- Highlight benefits and outcomes: Focus on the impact of your message, which can be understood universally, rather than the complex processes behind it.

- Incorporate stories and examples: Illustrate your points with stories or examples that embody the concepts without relying heavily on technical language.

- Layer information: Start with a broad overview before delving into specifics, allowing the audience to grasp the fundamental ideas first.

- Expert quotes and testimonials: Incorporate insights from recognized experts in your field. This adds credibility while also breaking down complex ideas into more digestible pieces.

Navigating the fine line between simplicity and expertise does not mean dumbing down your message but rather enhancing its reach and impact. By consciously choosing language that resonates across spectrums of knowledge and experience, you invite a wider audience into the conversation, fostering an inclusive environment where ideas flourish. In doing so, you not only amplify your message but also cultivate a community of informed, engaged, and inspired individuals, united by a shared understanding.

Elevator Pitches: Conveying Value in Seconds

In the high-speed elevator of opportunity, your pitch is the key that can unlock doors. An elevator pitch, succinct and potent, distils the essence of your business value into a few, impactful seconds. It's not merely a brief description of what you do; it's an artful synthesis of your mission, your method, and your magic, designed to captivate and convince within the span of a fleeting elevator ride.

The Essence of an Elevator Pitch

The core of an elevator pitch lies in its brevity and precision. It's an orchestrated effort to encapsulate your business's value proposition in a timeframe that respects the listener's attention span while leaving them wanting more. The importance of this concise communication format cannot be overstated. In a world where attention is fragmented and time is at a premium, the ability to express your business's value quickly and effectively can open doors to new opportunities, partnerships, and growth avenues.

Structure of an Effective Pitch

A well-composed elevator pitch follows a clear, compelling structure, inviting the listener on a quick yet complete journey through the heart of your business. The components include:

- Problem: Start by identifying a problem or need that is both relatable and pressing. This sets the stage by engaging the listener's interest and empathy.

- Solution: Introduce your product or service as the solution, focusing on how it addresses the problem in a unique or superior way.

- Unique Value Proposition (UVP): Highlight what sets your solution apart from others. This could be your innovative approach, exceptional service, or a key feature that offers distinct benefits.

- Call to Action (CTA): Conclude with a clear, motivating invitation for the listener to take the next step, whether it's visiting your website, scheduling a meeting, or simply expressing interest in learning more.

Practicing Your Pitch

Polishing your elevator pitch to ensure it's delivered with confidence and clarity requires practice. Here are some strategies to refine your pitch:

- Rehearse Out Loud: Practice your pitch out loud, either in front of a mirror or to a trusted colleague or friend. This helps you get comfortable with the flow and timing.

- Time Yourself: Use a stopwatch to ensure your pitch stays within the 30-60-second sweet spot. This helps you identify parts that may need trimming or condensing.

- Refine for Clarity: Simplify your language to ensure your message is easily understood. Avoid jargon or technical terms that might confuse the listener.

- Seek Feedback: Encourage honest feedback from those who listen to your pitch. Use their insights to make necessary adjustments for clarity, interest, and impact.

Real-world Examples

Examining successful elevator pitches provides valuable lessons on crafting your own. Consider the pitch that secured initial funding for Dropbox. It focused on a universal problem — the difficulty of working across multiple computers and losing USB drives. The solution was elegantly simple: a folder that syncs by itself. The pitch was direct, relatable, and highlighted a clear benefit, making it a compelling case for potential investors.

Another example comes from Airbnb's initial pitch, which centred on the problem of finding affordable, safe, and unique lodging options while traveling. The solution? A platform that lets people rent out their spaces to travellers. The UVP was clear — an authentic travel experience at a fraction of the cost of a hotel, plus the opportunity for hosts to earn extra income. The pitch successfully captured the essence of Airbnb's business model, appealing to both travellers and potential hosts.

These examples underscore the importance of a well-structured pitch that concisely communicates the problem, solution, and unique value proposition. They also highlight the effectiveness of rehearsing and refining your pitch to ensure it resonates with your intended audience.

Crafting an elevator pitch that succinctly conveys the value of your business is an essential skill in today's fast-paced world. By focusing on a relatable problem, presenting a clear solution, and highlighting your unique value proposition, you can create a pitch that not only captures attention but also opens doors to new opportunities. Practice and refinement, guided by constructive feedback, will ensure your pitch is delivered with the confidence and clarity necessary to make a lasting impression.

Communicating with Confidence: How to Overcome Public Speaking Anxiety

The mere thought of standing before an audience, all eyes fixed expectantly, can make the most seasoned professionals experience a spine-tingling sensation. This nervous anticipation isn't just common; it's a shared human experience. Public speaking anxiety, deeply rooted in our psyche, often stems from a fear of judgment, failure, or the unknown. The impact of this anxiety is not insignificant—it can cloud our clarity, dampen our enthusiasm, and, in severe cases, impede our career progression. However, by understanding its origins and employing targeted strategies, we can transform this nervous energy into a dynamic force that propels our communication.

Exploring the Roots of Public Speaking Anxiety

To navigate through the fog of public speaking anxiety, we first need to understand its landscape. Often, this anxiety is not about the act of speaking itself but about the perceived stakes of the situation. It's the fear of not meeting expectations—our own or those of our audience—that amplifies pressure. Contributing factors include:

- Past experiences, where previous encounters with public speaking, whether negative or positive, shape our anticipations.
- Lack of familiarity, where unfamiliarity with the audience or content increases uncertainty.
- Personality traits, where individuals who identify as perfectionists or introverts might experience heightened anxiety.

Acknowledging these roots is the first step towards addressing public speaking anxiety, not as an insurmountable barrier but as a challenge to be overcome.

Strategies for Building Confidence

Confidence in public speaking, much like any skill, can be developed. The foundation of this development lies in thorough preparation and a deep belief in one's message. Strategies to build this confidence include:

- In-depth preparation: Familiarize yourself with your content until it feels like second nature. This reduces the fear of forgetting or stumbling over your words.

- Know your audience: Understanding who you are speaking to allows you to tailor your message, making it more relevant and engaging.

- Practice: Rehearse your speech in a setting that simulates the real environment as closely as possible. This could involve practicing in the actual room or recording yourself to critique later.

These strategies not only prepare you for the task at hand but also instil a sense of readiness that is crucial for confidence.

Techniques for Managing Anxiety

Managing anxiety in the moment requires a toolkit of strategies that can be deployed to calm nerves and maintain focus. These techniques include:

- Breathing exercises: Deep, controlled breathing helps reduce physiological symptoms of anxiety, such as a racing heart or shaking hands.

- Focusing strategies: Concentrate on your message and the value it brings to your audience rather than on yourself. This shifts the perspective from self-consciousness to service.

- Positive self-talk: Replace negative thoughts with affirmations. Remind yourself of your preparedness and your message's importance.

Employing these techniques helps keep anxiety at bay, allowing your confidence and clarity to shine through.

Learning from Experience

The path to mastering public speaking is paved with experience. Each opportunity to speak is a stepping stone, offering valuable lessons that contribute to growth. The role of experience and feedback in this journey includes:

- Reflective practice: After each speaking engagement, take time to reflect on what went well and what could be improved. This reflection turns experience into actionable insights.

- Seeking constructive feedback: Encourage feedback from trusted colleagues or mentors. Objective insights can highlight strengths and pinpoint areas for development.

- Incremental challenges: Gradually increase the complexity and stakes of your speaking engagements. This could mean starting with small, familiar audiences and progressively moving to larger, more diverse groups.

This process of continuous learning and adaptation is key to diminishing public speaking anxiety over time. Each experience, analysed and built upon, contributes to a deeper understanding and greater confidence.

Public speaking, for many, is a daunting endeavour, shadowed by anxiety and self-doubt. However, by uncovering the roots of this anxiety, employing strategies to build confidence, mastering techniques to manage nervousness, and embracing each speaking opportunity as a learning experience, we can transform public speaking from a source of fear to a platform for influence. Through preparation, practice, and persistence, the journey from anxiety to assurance is not only possible but profoundly rewarding.

Structuring Your Presentations for Maximum Engagement

Crafting a presentation that captivates and retains the audience's attention from start to finish is akin to constructing a bridge. Every element, from the foundational concept to the keystone of interaction, must be meticulously placed to ensure a smooth passage for your audience from curiosity to understanding. This section delves into the crafting of presentations that not only inform but also engage, creating a memorable experience for every listener.

Components of an Engaging Presentation

EFFECTIVE COMMUNICATION SKILLS

A presentation that truly engages an audience is multi-dimensional, incorporating various elements that work together to maintain interest and encourage interaction.

- Storytelling: Weaving your message into a narrative keeps the audience invested in the outcome. The story's structure – with a clear beginning, middle, and end – provides a familiar framework that helps listeners follow along.

- Visuals: Strategic use of visuals can illustrate complex ideas more effectively than words alone. This includes slides, charts, images, and videos that complement your narrative and highlight key points.

- Audience Interaction: Incorporating moments where the audience can participate transforms passive listeners into active participants. This could be through direct questions, live polls, or even brief group discussions.

Designing Your Presentation

Designing an impactful presentation requires careful consideration of the flow of information and the use of visual and interactive elements to complement your narrative.

- Start with a hook: Begin with an intriguing question, a surprising fact, or a compelling story that relates to your topic. This initial hook draws in your audience and sets the tone for the presentation.

- Organize information logically: Arrange your content in a logical order that builds on each concept. Use clear transitions between sections to guide your audience through the presentation.

- Simplify your slides: Keep slides clean and focused, using bullet points or short phrases rather than dense paragraphs. Each slide should support your spoken words, not replace them.

- Incorporate variety: Break up the flow with different types of content. Switch between stories, facts, visuals, and interactive elements to keep the presentation dynamic and prevent monotony.

Engagement Techniques

Maintaining audience engagement throughout your presentation can be challenging, but various techniques can help keep your listeners active and involved.

- Live Polls: Tools like live polling apps allow you to pose questions to your audience and see the results in real-time. This not only adds interactivity but also provides valuable feedback on your audience's understanding and opinions.

- Questions and Answers: Allocating time for Q&A sessions encourages audience members to engage directly with the content. Prompt questions at the start to give listeners time to formulate their thoughts.

- Interactive Elements: Incorporating elements like quizzes or brief group discussions can break up the presentation and give the audience a chance to process and apply what they've learned.

Evaluating Presentation Effectiveness

Determining the success of your presentation relies on both immediate feedback from the audience and self-assessment.

- Immediate Feedback: Observe the audience's body language and engagement levels throughout the presentation. Are they leaning forward, making eye contact, and participating? Or are they distracted and disengaged?

- Post-Presentation Surveys: Distribute brief surveys or feedback forms at the end of your presentation. Ask specific questions about what the audience found most engaging or areas they felt needed improvement.

- Self-Assessment: Review a recording of your presentation or reflect on your performance. Consider the pacing, clarity, and use of visuals and interaction. Recognise areas for improvement and strategies to enhance future presentations.

By integrating these components and techniques into your presentation design, you create an experience that engages, informs, and resonates with your audience. The goal is not just to share information but to foster an environment of active learning and participation, ensuring that your message not only reaches your audience but truly connects with them.

Mastering Meetings: Facilitation and Participation Techniques

Meetings, the linchpins of corporate communication, vary widely in their efficiency and effectiveness. Skilful meeting facilitation and active participation can transform these gatherings from time-consuming obligations into catalysts for innovation, decision-making, and team cohesion. This section explores the nuanced roles of facilitators and participants, alongside strategies for navigating meeting dynamics and ensuring actionable outcomes.

Effective Meeting Facilitation

The facilitator's role extends beyond mere agenda-setting to shaping the meeting's tone, pace, and inclusivity. A facilitator ensures that meetings are not only productive but also focused and respectful of participants' time and contributions. Key aspects include:

- Preparation: Well before the meeting, a facilitator should outline clear objectives, prepare an agenda, and distribute it to participants. This preparation sets the stage for a focused discussion.

- Time Management: Keeping the meeting on track and within the allocated time respects participants' schedules and maintains engagement. This may involve tactfully steering conversations back to the agenda and limiting divergences.

- Inclusivity: Ensuring that all voices are heard is crucial. This might involve inviting quieter members to share their thoughts or mediating when discussions become dominated by a few voices.

- Environment: Creating a comfortable and open environment encourages open dialogue and creative thinking. This could be as simple as arranging seats in a circle to promote equality or starting the meeting with a positive note to set an engaging tone.

Participation Strategies

Effective participation in meetings is equally important, contributing to the meeting's overall productivity and outcomes. Participants can enhance the quality of meetings by:

- Active Listening: This involves fully concentrating on the speaker, understanding their message, providing feedback, and withholding judgment. Active listeners contribute to a culture of respect and understanding within the team.

- Constructive Feedback: Offering insights and suggestions constructively fosters a positive and collaborative atmosphere. It's about adding value, not just voicing dissent.

- Clear Communication: Expressing ideas clearly and concisely respects the time of all participants and aids in the smooth flow of information. This includes being prepared to discuss agenda items and asking clarifying questions when necessary.

Managing Challenging Dynamics

Meetings can sometimes veer into difficult territory, with conflicts, dominance, or disengagement hindering progress. Techniques to manage these dynamics include:

- Addressing Conflicts: When disagreements arise, acknowledge them openly and work towards a resolution that respects all viewpoints. This might involve breaking down the issue to understand its root cause or seeking a compromise that aligns with the meeting's objectives.

- Balancing Dominance: Should one or two voices begin to overshadow the conversation, a facilitator can gently intervene, thanking them for their contributions but also reminding the group of the value of diverse perspectives. Directing questions to quieter members can help rebalance the discussion.

- Re-engaging Participants: Signs of disengagement, such as

distracted behaviour or silence, may require a change in the meeting's direction. This could involve introducing a new topic, taking a short break, or incorporating an interactive element to revive interest and participation.

Follow-up and Accountability

The effectiveness of a meeting is ultimately measured by the actions that follow. Ensuring that decisions lead to outcomes involves:

- Clear Action Items: Conclude meetings with a summary of decisions made, tasks assigned, and deadlines established. This clarity helps participants understand their responsibilities and the next steps.

- Documentation: Keeping a record of the meeting's key points, decisions, and action items aids in accountability and provides a reference for those unable to attend.

- Follow-Up: Facilitators or designated team members should follow up on action items, providing support where necessary and addressing any roadblocks encountered. This follow-up ensures momentum is maintained and objectives are met.

Meetings, when conducted effectively, are more than just a routine part of corporate life; they are opportunities for collaboration, innovation, and progress. By honing facilitation and participation skills, managing meeting dynamics proactively, and emphasizing follow-up and accountability, teams can ensure that their gatherings are not only productive but also a positive, engaging, and integral part of their success.

Handling Difficult Conversations with Grace and Strategy

Navigating the waters of difficult conversations requires a mindful blend of preparation, emotional intelligence, and the ability to maintain composure under pressure. These conversations, whether they involve delivering unwelcome news, addressing performance issues, or negotiating conflicts, test our communication skills to their limits. Yet, they also present opportunities for growth, deeper understanding, and strengthened relationships when approached with the right mindset and techniques.

Preparing for Difficult Conversations

Entering a challenging discussion without proper preparation is akin to setting sail in stormy seas without a compass. Preparation anchors you, providing direction and confidence. Begin by defining the objective of the conversation. What outcome are you hoping to achieve? Understanding this helps shape your approach and keeps the conversation focused. Gather all necessary information and anticipate possible reactions or questions. This preparation allows you to approach the conversation with clarity and purpose, ensuring you're not caught off guard by unexpected developments.

- Outline your main points to stay on track.
- Consider the best time and setting for the conversation, aiming for privacy and minimal interruptions.
- Reflect on your own emotions regarding the topic to manage them effectively during the discussion.

Navigating Emotional Responses

Emotions can run high during challenging conversations, both in yourself and the person you're speaking with. Managing these emotional responses is crucial to maintaining a constructive dialogue. Begin by acknowledging emotions without letting them steer the conversation. For instance, if frustration arises, recognize it, but refocus on the conversation's objective. Techniques such as deep breathing or pausing before responding can help keep emotions in check.

- Practice active listening, showing empathy and understanding towards the other person's perspective.
- Keep your tone and body language neutral, avoiding defensive or aggressive postures.
- If emotions escalate, suggest a brief pause to allow everyone time to calm down.

EFFECTIVE COMMUNICATION SKILLS

Communicating with Empathy and Assertiveness

Balancing empathy and assertiveness is the key to effective communication in tough situations. Empathy involves genuinely trying to understand the other person's feelings and viewpoint, while assertiveness means clearly and respectfully expressing your own. This balance ensures the conversation remains respectful and productive, even when discussing difficult topics.

- Use "I" statements to convey your emotions and requirements without blaming or accusing the other person.
- Ask open-ended questions to encourage dialogue and show you value the other person's input.
- Clearly state your needs or the outcome you're seeking from the conversation but remain open to finding mutual solutions.

Learning from Difficult Conversations

Every challenging conversation offers a chance for personal and professional growth. Reflecting on these experiences can provide valuable insights into your communication style, emotional triggers, and conflict resolution skills. After the conversation, take some time to assess what went well and what could have been improved. Consider the following:

- Was the objective of the conversation achieved? If not, why?
- How did you manage your emotions and those of the other person?
- What did you learn from this experience that could help in future conversations?

This reflection not only enhances your communication skills but also helps build resilience, making future difficult conversations less daunting.

In navigating the complexities of challenging discussions, remember that the goal is not to win but to communicate effectively, fostering understanding and finding solutions. By preparing thoroughly, managing emotions wisely, balancing empathy with assertiveness, and learning from each encounter, you can transform difficult conversations from feared events into opportunities for meaningful dialogue and growth.

As we close this chapter, it's clear that the art of communication extends far beyond the exchange of information. It's about connecting with others on a deeper level, navigating complexities with grace, and emerging stronger from the experience. These skills, honed through practice and reflection, not only enhance our professional interactions but enrich our personal relationships as well. Looking ahead, we'll continue to explore the multifaceted nature of effective communication, building on these foundations to tackle new challenges and seize growth opportunities.

Chapter Three

Beyond the Words: The Subtleties of Listening

Listening, at its core, is an invisible thread that weaves through the very fabric of our interactions, holding the potential to either strengthen or unravel the connections we strive to build. It's easy to overlook, yet its impact is profound, influencing not just the outcomes of our conversations but the quality of our relationships and the effectiveness of our leadership. We often assume that hearing equates to listening. However, true listening is far more complex and challenging than simply processing sound. It entails decoding messages, interpreting tones, and understanding contexts—all while navigating our own biases and emotional responses.

The Psychology of Listening: Why It's Harder Than You Think

Cognitive Biases and Their Impact

Cognitive biases shape our perception of the world, influencing how we interpret information and interact with others. These mental shortcuts, while useful in processing vast amounts of information, can distort our listening. Confirmation bias, for example, leads us to favour information that aligns with our existing beliefs, ignoring or dismissing what doesn't. This can significantly impact our ability to listen openly and objectively, especially in discussions that challenge our viewpoints.

- Strategies to mitigate bias: Actively seek diverse perspectives and question your initial reactions to information. This can help counteract the influence of biases on your listening.

The Multitasking Myth

The modern workplace often lauds the ability to multitask. Yet, the belief that we can effectively juggle multiple tasks is a myth, particularly when it comes to listening. Each task competes for a portion of our cognitive resources, diminishing our capacity to process and understand information fully. Listening while checking emails, for instance, compromises our ability to grasp the nuances of the conversation, leading to misunderstandings and overlooked details.

- Single-task focus: Prioritize listening by eliminating distractions. This means putting away devices and giving speakers your undivided attention, ensuring you capture the full essence of their message.

Emotional Noise

Our emotions act as a filter through which we perceive and interpret conversations. Strong emotions, whether positive or negative, can obscure our judgment and impede our ability to listen effectively. For instance, anxiety about a work project might make us more likely to perceive neutral feedback as criticism, affecting our response and the conversation's outcome.

- Managing emotions: Recognize when emotions might be influencing your listening. Techniques such as deep breathing or pausing to reflect before responding can help maintain objectivity and openness in discussions.

Overcoming Psychological Barriers

Recognizing and addressing the psychological barriers to effective listening is crucial for improving our communication skills. This involves being mindful of our biases, managing our emotional responses, and resisting the urge to multitask during conversations.

- Practice summarizing what the other person has said before responding to ensure you have accurately understood their message. This exercise can enhance your listening skills and demonstrate your engagement with the speaker.

- Reflection: After conversations, especially challenging ones, reflect on your listening. Consider what barriers might have affected your understanding and how you can address these in future interactions.

Effective listening is an intricate skill, influenced by a myriad of factors beyond our immediate control. Yet, by understanding these influences and actively working to mitigate their impact, we can improve not only our ability to listen but also our overall effectiveness as communicators. In doing so, we open the door to deeper connections, enhanced understanding, and more meaningful interactions in both our personal and professional lives.

Active Listening in Negotiations: The Key to Unlocking Value

In the intricate dance of negotiation, where every word and pause carries weight, active listening emerges as a pivotal force. This nuanced form of listening goes beyond the mere act of hearing words; it involves a deep engagement with the speaker's message, both spoken and unspoken, to uncover underlying interests and create mutual value. Active listening in negotiations is not merely a passive reception of information but a dynamic interaction that fosters understanding, trust, and collaboration.

Active Listening as a Negotiation Tool

Active listening acts as a beacon, illuminating the path to compromise and agreement in negotiations. It allows negotiators to dig beneath the surface of stated positions to unearth the real needs and interests of the parties involved. This understanding is crucial for crafting solutions that offer genuine value to all sides. By focusing intently on the speaker, acknowledging their points, and reflecting on their message, negotiators can validate the other party's perspective, creating a foundation for open dialogue and creative problem-solving.

- Validation of concerns: Demonstrates understanding and respect for the other party's viewpoints, encouraging more open communication.

- Clarification of needs: Helps in accurately identifying the needs and interests underlying the positions of negotiating parties.

Techniques for Enhancing Listening in Negotiations

Several techniques can enhance one's ability to engage in active listening during negotiations, turning conversations into opportunities for finding mutually beneficial outcomes.

- Paraphrasing: Reiterate the speaker's points in your own words, confirming your understanding and demonstrating attentiveness.

- Asking open-ended questions: Encourage elaboration and clarification, providing deeper insights into the speaker's perspective.

- Maintaining eye contact: Signals engagement and interest, fostering a more connected communication environment.

- Note-taking: Capturing key points can aid in understanding and reference during later stages of the negotiation.

These techniques not only facilitate a deeper understanding of the other party's position but also signal respect and willingness to engage constructively, setting a positive tone for the negotiation.

Building Trust Through Listening

Trust is the cornerstone of effective negotiations, and active listening is one of its main architects. By genuinely engaging with the speaker, showing empathy, and validating their concerns, negotiators can build a bridge of trust that supports the weight of compromise and agreement. This trust paves the way for more open and honest exchanges, reducing defensiveness and fostering a collaborative spirit. It signals a commitment to understanding and addressing the needs of all parties, creating a fertile ground for innovative solutions to emerge.

- Reducing defensiveness: Creates a safer environment for open dialogue, minimizing barriers to understanding.

- Encouraging reciprocity: Often leads to reciprocal listening efforts from the other party, enhancing mutual understanding.

Case Studies

Examples underscore the transformative power of active listening in negotiations. In one notable instance, a major corporation faced a deadlock with a key supplier over pricing terms. The negotiations were tense, with both sides firmly entrenched in their positions. By implementing active listening techniques, the corporation's negotiation team was able to uncover the supplier's underlying concerns about stability and long-term collaboration. This insight shifted the focus from price to partnership, leading to an agreement that provided value and security for both parties.

In another case, a startup was negotiating a crucial investment deal with potential backers. The initial discussions were challenging, with significant gaps in valuation and terms. The startup's founders employed active listening, paying close attention to the investors' feedback and questions. This approach revealed the investors' concerns about market risk and the startup's growth trajectory. Armed with this understanding, the founders adjusted their pitch to address these concerns directly, successfully securing the investment on favourable terms.

These cases illustrate how active listening can unlock value in negotiations, transforming potential conflicts into opportunities for agreement. By focusing on understanding and addressing the fundamental needs and interests of all parties, negotiators can navigate complex discussions more effectively, leading to outcomes that offer genuine benefits and strengthen relationships.

Active listening, with its emphasis on empathy, understanding, and trust, proves to be a critical skill in the negotiator's toolkit. It requires patience, attentiveness, and a genuine commitment to engaging with the other party's perspective. In the realm of negotiations, where success is measured by the ability to find common ground and build lasting agreements, mastering the art of active listening can be a decisive factor. Through its application, negotiators can navigate the intricacies of dialogue, uncover hidden opportunities for compromise, and forge agreements that stand the test of time.

Listening for What's Not Said: Nonverbal Cues and Silent Signals

In the realm of effective communication, the unspoken often carries as much weight—if not more—than the words exchanged. Nonverbal cues, those silent signals conveyed through body language, facial expressions, and even the absence of sound, provide a deeper insight into the true sentiments and intentions behind a message. Recognizing and interpreting these cues is a nuanced skill, one that enhances our understanding and responsiveness in interactions, fostering connections that are both meaningful and authentic.

The Importance of Nonverbal Cues

Nonverbal communication forms a significant portion of our daily interactions, often occurring subconsciously. These cues, from a subtle shift in posture to the briefest flicker of emotion across the face, speak volumes about a person's true feelings and thoughts. In professional settings, where words are measured and conversations are laden with strategic intent, nonverbal cues become invaluable in decoding the complete message. They offer clues to a speaker's confidence, sincerity, and receptiveness, guiding us in our responses and strategies.

- Enhancing empathy: Observing nonverbal cues allows us to better empathize with the speaker, tailoring our communication to address their emotions and concerns effectively.

- Detecting incongruences: Discrepancies between verbal and nonverbal messages often indicate hidden reservations or unexpressed objections, which are crucial to identify and address in negotiations and team interactions.

Interpreting Silence and Pauses

Silence, in its myriad forms, communicates as powerfully as words. Pauses in conversation can signal contemplation, resistance, or a plea for space to process information. The context and accompanying nonverbal cues are essential in interpreting these silences accurately. For instance, a prolonged pause following a proposal might suggest hesitation or concern, inviting further exploration. Alternatively, a brief silence before answering a question might indicate careful consideration, signifying the importance of the response.

- Contextual interpretation: Consider the context and flow of the conversation to accurately interpret the meaning behind silences and pauses.

- Responsive strategies: Use these moments as opportunities to offer clarification, probe gently for more information, or simply give the speaker the time they need to articulate their thoughts.

Reading Between the Lines

Detecting and interpreting the unsaid messages and emotions conveyed through nonverbal cues requires keen observation and sensitivity. These silent signals often reveal the underlying dynamics of a conversation, from power imbalances to unspoken agreements. For example, a team member's avoidance of eye contact during a feedback session might signal discomfort or disagreement, necessitating a more nuanced approach to ensure their openness and engagement.

- Observing patterns: Pay attention to patterns in nonverbal behaviour, as these can provide consistent indicators of a person's feelings and reactions.

- Cross-referencing cues: Combine multiple nonverbal signals, such as facial expressions, posture, and vocal tone, to form a more accurate interpretation of the speaker's state of mind.

Enhancing Observation Skills

Developing the ability to accurately observe and interpret nonverbal cues is a skill that can significantly enhance our listening capabilities. This involves not only paying attention to the speaker's body language and facial expressions but also being mindful of our own nonverbal signals, which can influence the flow and outcome of the conversation. The following exercises can help sharpen these observation skills:

- Focused observation: During conversations, consciously direct your attention to the speaker's nonverbal cues. Afterward, reflect on what you observed and how it aligned with or contrasted their verbal communication.

- Silent communication exercises: Engage in exercises where

verbal communication is restricted, relying solely on nonverbal cues to convey messages. This can heighten awareness of the variety and subtlety of nonverbal communication.

- Feedback loop: Seek feedback on your interpretations of nonverbal cues from trusted colleagues or mentors. This will create valuable insights into the accuracy of your observations and areas for improvement.

By honing the ability to listen for what's not said and to read the silent signals that permeate our interactions, we can achieve a deeper understanding and connection with those around us. This skill empowers us to respond more effectively and empathetically, bridging gaps in communication and fostering environments where collaboration and trust thrive. In the intricate dance of dialogue, where every gesture and pause has meaning, our ability to interpret these nonverbal cues becomes not just an asset but a necessity, enriching our interactions and amplifying our impact as communicators.

Empathic Listening: The Path to Deeper Business Relationships

In the intricate tapestry of business communications, empathic listening emerges as a golden thread, binding conversations with depth and warmth that fosters genuine connection and collaboration. Unlike the simple act of hearing, empathic listening invites us into the emotional landscape of our conversational partners, allowing us to perceive not just the words, but the sentiments and intentions woven between them. This level of understanding is transformative, laying the groundwork for relationships that transcend the transactional and delve into the truly meaningful.

Defining Empathic Listening

Empathic listening is an elevated form of engagement where the listener fully immerses themselves in the speaker's perspective, feeling with the speaker and understanding their emotional state as well as their verbal message. This goes beyond sympathetic listening where one may feel for the speaker but not fully engage with their emotional experience. Empathic listening involves a conscious effort to set aside one's own thoughts and judgments to be fully present with the speaker, creating a safe space for true expression.

- Active Engagement: This requires the listener's full participation, using verbal affirmations and nonverbal cues to show understanding and empathy.
- Reflective Feedback: Part of empathic listening involves reflecting on what has been said to confirm understanding, often mirroring the speaker's emotions.

The Role of Empathy in Business

The business world, often criticized for its emphasis on results over relationships, is ripe for the transformative power of empathic listening. At its core, every business interaction is a human interaction, laden with emotions, aspirations, and vulnerabilities. By embracing empathic listening, leaders, managers, and team members can build more profound connections, leading to enhanced trust, improved collaboration, and a culture that values each individual's contribution and well-being.

- Trust Building: Empathic listening demonstrates respect and concern for colleagues and clients, laying a foundation of trust that is essential for effective collaboration.
- Conflict Resolution: It allows for the acknowledgment and validation of differing perspectives, facilitating more compassionate and effective conflict resolution strategies.
- Innovation Encouragement: In an environment where individuals feel heard and valued, there is a greater inclination to share ideas freely, fostering innovation and creativity.

Practicing Empathic Listening

Developing the skill of empathic listening requires intention and practice. It is a journey of moving beyond one's own perspective to truly understand and connect with others on an emotional level. Here are some practical steps and exercises to refine empathic listening skills:

- **Mindful Presence:** Begin by cultivating a practice of mindfulness, training yourself to be fully present in each interaction without distraction.

- **Emotional Vocabulary Expansion:** Work on expanding your emotional vocabulary to more accurately reflect the speaker's feelings and experiences.

- **Listening Exercises:** Engage in exercises designed to enhance empathic understanding, such as listening to a colleague without interrupting or offering solutions, focusing instead on understanding their emotional journey.

- **Feedback Seeking:** After conversations, ask for feedback on your listening skills, focusing on areas of improvement to deepen your empathic engagement.

Overcoming Challenges to Empathic Listening

While the benefits of empathic listening are substantial, several challenges can impede its practice. Recognizing and addressing these challenges is crucial for anyone looking to harness the power of empathic listening in their professional and personal lives.

- **Personal Bias Recognition:** We all carry biases that can color our perceptions. Acknowledging these biases allows us to listen more openly and without judgment.

- **Emotional Overwhelm Management:** At times, empathic listening can lead to emotional overwhelm, especially when dealing with intense or difficult emotions. Learning to manage one's own emotional responses is key to maintaining effectiveness as an empathic listener.

- **Time Constraints Acknowledgment:** In fast-paced business environments, taking the time to listen empathically can seem like a luxury. However, recognizing the long-term benefits of building deeper connections and understanding can justify the investment of time and attention.

Empathic listening represents a profound shift in how we engage with others, moving beyond the exchange of information to a deeper sharing of experiences and emotions. It is a skill that not only enhances our effectiveness as communicators but also enriches our relationships, opening up new avenues for collaboration, innovation, and mutual understanding. In the realm of business, where relationships are the bedrock of success, empathic listening emerges not just as a tool, but as a guiding principle, shaping interactions that are not only productive but also deeply human.

Feedback: Giving and Receiving Constructively

In the dynamic landscape of business communication, feedback stands as a pivotal mechanism for growth, learning, and innovation. This dual-faceted tool, involving both the offering and acceptance of insights, is integral to refining processes, enhancing skills, and fostering an environment of continuous improvement. Recognizing its value, however, is merely the first step. The true challenge lies in navigating the delicate balance of delivering feedback that is both constructive and actionable, and in receiving it with an open mind, poised for growth.

The Dual Role of Feedback in Communication

Feedback serves as a mirror, reflecting the impact of our actions and words from perspectives outside our own. This reflection is crucial not just for individual development but for the collective evolution of teams and organizations. On one hand, giving feedback is about guiding others toward their potential, and shining light on opportunities for enhancement. On the other, receiving feedback is an exercise in humility and growth, acknowledging that there is always room for improvement.

- Mutual growth: Both roles are instrumental in creating a cycle of positive change and development.
- Enhanced understanding: Feedback opens channels of communication, clarifying expectations, and fostering deeper mutual understanding.

Constructive Feedback Techniques

Navigating the art of providing feedback that is constructive rather than critical requires tact, empathy, and clarity. The goal is to encourage, not discourage, to build up rather than tear down.

- Focus on behaviour, not personality: Direct comments towards actions and their outcomes, avoiding attributions to personal traits. For example, instead of saying someone is disorganized, point to specific instances where a more structured approach could have enhanced efficiency.

- Be specific and objective: Ground your feedback in concrete examples and objective observations. This specificity not only makes the feedback more actionable but also helps depersonalize it, making it easier to receive.

- Offer solutions or next steps: Pair critiques with suggestions for improvement or potential solutions. This constructive approach transforms feedback from a critique into a roadmap for development.

- Timing and setting matter: Choose an appropriate time and private setting for feedback discussions, ensuring the recipient is in a receptive state.

Receiving Feedback with Openness

The flip side of the feedback coin—receiving it with grace and a willingness to learn—can be equally challenging. It requires setting aside ego and defensiveness to see feedback as a gift, an opportunity for growth.

- Listen fully before responding: Resist the urge to formulate a response or defense while the feedback is still being delivered. Listening fully helps ensure you understand the feedback's intent and content.

- Seek clarification: If certain points are unclear, ask for specific examples or suggestions. This proactive approach not only clarifies the feedback but also demonstrates your commitment to improvement.

- Express appreciation: Irrespective of whether you agree with the feedback, acknowledging the effort and courage it takes to offer feedback fosters a positive culture around it.

- Reflect and act: Take time to reflect on the feedback received, assessing its validity and how it can be used for personal or professional development. Then, create an action plan for implementation.

Creating a Culture of Feedback

Cultivating an environment where feedback is regularly exchanged, valued, and acted upon can transform the fabric of an organization, making it more agile, transparent, and aligned.

- Lead by example: Leaders and managers should model both giving and receiving feedback openly and constructively. Their behaviour sets the tone for the entire organization.

- Regular, structured opportunities: Incorporate feedback into regular operational rhythms, such as performance reviews, project debriefs, and one-on-one meetings. This regularity normalizes feedback, making it an expected part of organizational life.

- Training and resources: Provide training and resources on effective feedback techniques. Equipping team members with the skills to give and receive feedback constructively enhances the quality of interactions.

- Celebrate the process: Recognize and celebrate instances where feedback leads to positive outcomes. This recognition reinforces the value of feedback and encourages its continued exchange.

In navigating the complexities of giving and receiving feedback, we find opportunities for growth, resilience, and connection. By approaching feedback with intention, empathy, and openness, we not only enhance our capabilities but also contribute to the development of a culture that values continuous improvement and mutual respect. In this culture, feedback is not a moment of critique but a continuous dialogue, a shared journey toward excellence and understanding. Through constructive feedback practices, we unlock the potential within ourselves and others, fostering an environment where learning and growth are not just encouraged but embedded in the very essence of our interactions.

Listening Challenges in Digital Communication

The landscape of digital communication, vast and varied, introduces unique hurdles to the fundamental act of listening. The reliance on technology-mediated interactions strip away layers of context and nuance, challenging our ability to listen effectively. This environment demands a re-evaluation of our listening strategies, urging us to adapt and innovate to maintain the integrity of our connections.

Unique Challenges of Digital Listening

Digital platforms, while breaking down geographical barriers, erect new ones in the realm of communication. The richness of face-to-face interaction, laden with visual cues and the immediacy of response, often becomes diluted in digital exchanges. Text-based communication, devoid of tone and timing, leaves much to interpretation, increasing the potential for misunderstanding. Audio and video calls, though closer to mimicking in-person interaction, are not immune to challenges; audio lags, video freezes, and the disembodied nature of voices can disrupt the flow of communication, hindering our ability to listen and respond with the same level of engagement and understanding as we might in physical settings.

- Text Interpretation: The lack of vocal inflection and body language in text-based messages can lead to misinterpretation of tone, intent, and emotion.
- Technology Limitations: Technical issues such as poor connection quality can disrupt audio and visual cues, making it harder to maintain focus and interpret messages correctly.

Enhancing Listening in Virtual Meetings

As virtual meetings become a staple in the modern workplace, refining our listening skills in this context is crucial. Strategies to amplify our listening capacity in digital settings hinge on both technological solutions and personal discipline.

- **Use of Headphones:** Employing headphones can reduce background noise and enhance audio clarity, minimizing distractions and allowing for better focus on the conversation.

- **Active Participation:** Engage actively by nodding, maintaining eye contact with the camera, and using the chat function to pose questions or express agreement, fostering a more interactive and engaging virtual environment.

- **Pre-meeting Preparation:** Familiarizing yourself with the meeting agenda and participants beforehand can help you tune in more effectively, making it easier to follow the discussion and identify key points.

Interpreting Digital Nonverbal Cues

In the digital realm, nonverbal communication transforms. The cues we rely on in face-to-face interactions take new forms, requiring a recalibration of our interpretive lens.

- **The tone of Voice in Audio Calls:** Variations in pitch, pace, and volume can offer insights into the speaker's emotional state and level of engagement, serving as valuable cues in the absence of visual feedback.

- **Timing of Responses in Text-Based Communication:** The speed or delay in responding can indicate the other party's level of interest or urgency concerning the topic, though it's important to consider technological and personal factors that might influence response time.

- **Visual Cues in Video Calls:** Facial expressions and gestures, though limited by the frame of the camera, remain potent indicators of nonverbal feedback. Paying attention to these cues can enhance understanding and empathy in virtual interactions.

Building Connection Through Digital Platforms

Fostering genuine connections in a digital setting demands creativity and intentionality. The absence of physical proximity necessitates a more deliberate approach to building rapport and ensuring meaningful interaction.

- Personalized Communication: Tailor your communication to the individual, incorporating personal touches such as addressing them by name or referencing past conversations to create a more personal connection.

- Regular Check-ins: Establish a routine of regular check-ins via video call or chat, not just about work tasks but also about sharing personal updates or successes, helping to maintain a sense of closeness and community.

- Virtual Team-Building Activities: Organize activities that can be done remotely, such as virtual coffee breaks or online team games, to foster team spirit and camaraderie in the absence of a physical shared space.

In navigating the digital landscape of communication, we confront a paradox; the very tools that facilitate connection across distances can also create barriers to the depth and quality of our interactions. The challenges of digital listening, from interpreting text-based messages devoid of tone to maintaining engagement in virtual meetings marred by technical glitches, test our adaptability and resolve. Yet, within these challenges lie opportunities—to redefine the boundaries of connection, to innovate in our methods of engagement, and to discover new depths of understanding and empathy. By embracing these strategies, we arm ourselves with the tools to not just navigate but thrive in the digital communication realm, ensuring that our capacity to listen, understand, and connect remains undiminished, irrespective of the medium.

Overcoming Selective Hearing in High-Stakes Situations

Selective hearing, a phenomenon where individuals subconsciously choose to hear and process only parts of the conversation that align with their preconceptions or desires, poses a significant barrier in high-stakes or emotionally charged environments. This selective engagement not only skews understanding but can also lead to missed opportunities and misinterpretations, potentially undermining relationships and decision-making processes.

Understanding Selective Hearing

At its core, selective hearing is not an act of deliberate ignorance but rather a subconscious defence mechanism. It often emerges in situations where the stakes are perceived as high, safeguarding individuals from information that might challenge their views or evoke discomfort. Emotionally charged discussions, where the potential for conflict looms large, are particularly prone to this phenomenon. Recognizing the occurrence of selective hearing is the first step towards addressing its impact, requiring a keen self-awareness and the willingness to confront one's own communication barriers.

Identifying Personal Biases

Personal biases act as the lens through which we view and interpret the world around us, heavily influencing our tendency towards selective hearing. These biases, rooted in our experiences, culture, and education, shape our perceptions and reactions, often unconsciously. To mitigate the influence of personal biases on listening:

- Reflect on past interactions: Analyse conversations where misunderstandings occurred. Identifying patterns can reveal biases that may have influenced your listening.

- Seek diverse perspectives: Expose yourself to viewpoints different from your own. This broadens your understanding and challenges your biases, fostering a more open and inclusive approach to listening.

- Engage in self-questioning: When you find yourself resisting or tuning out certain information, ask why. This introspection can uncover biases and pave the way for more objective listening.

Techniques for Full-Spectrum Listening

Full-spectrum listening involves engaging with and processing all elements of a message, including those that may be uncomfortable or challenging. This comprehensive approach to listening ensures a more balanced and complete understanding, vital in high-stakes situations. Techniques to enhance full-spectrum listening include:

- Active engagement: Beyond just hearing the words, engage with the speaker's emotions and nonverbal cues. This holistic engagement ensures a deeper understanding of the message.

- Pause before reacting: Allow yourself a moment to process information fully before formulating a response. This pause can prevent knee-jerk reactions based on selective hearing.

- Clarify and confirm: If certain points seem unclear or provoke a strong internal reaction, seek clarification. This not only ensures you've understood correctly but also demonstrates your commitment to comprehensive listening.

Case Studies on Overcoming Selective Hearing

In one notable instance, a project team faced significant delays and friction, attributed partly to selective hearing among its members. Each member had clung to their interpretations of the project's goals and methods, ignoring feedback and suggestions that contradicted their views. The breakthrough came when the team leader introduced a structured feedback session, employing techniques of full-spectrum listening. Members were encouraged to share their perspectives and, crucially, to listen to others without interruption. This exercise revealed the root causes of the misunderstandings and led to a renewed, unified approach that respected and incorporated diverse viewpoints.

Another case involved negotiations between a company and a key supplier. The initial meetings were unproductive, with each party selectively hearing only what supported their stance. Recognizing the impasse, the company's negotiation team applied full-spectrum listening techniques in subsequent discussions. They made a concerted effort to understand the supplier's concerns and constraints genuinely, leading to a breakthrough in negotiations. The final agreement reflected a deep mutual understanding, satisfying both parties' core needs and interests.

In both examples, overcoming selective hearing was pivotal in moving from deadlock to constructive outcomes. By adopting a mindset open to all facets of communication and employing strategies to counteract biases, the individuals and teams involved were able to navigate complex situations more effectively, leading to solutions that were mutually beneficial and sustainable.

Selective hearing, while a common obstacle in communication, particularly in high-stakes situations, is not insurmountable. Through increased self-awareness, a commitment to confronting personal biases, and the application of full-spectrum listening techniques, individuals can transcend selective engagement to achieve a deeper, more comprehensive understanding. This shift not only facilitates more effective communication but also fosters an environment where collaboration, innovation, and mutual respect can flourish, underscoring the critical role of listening in navigating the complexities of human interaction and decision-making.

The Role of Silence in Effective Communication

In the tapestry of human interaction, silence often carries a weight heavier than words, serving as a multifaceted tool in the art of communication. Its presence, far from indicating a void, can enrich the dialogue, providing space for reflection, understanding, and deeper connection. This section explores the strategic deployment of silence, its varied interpretations, and methods to harness its potential to enhance our communicative endeavours.

Silence as a Communication Tool

Silence, in its essence, is a powerful component of dialogue, offering a canvas upon which understanding and empathy can be drawn. It allows for the absorption of information, granting time for the listener to process spoken words, gauge the emotional undertones of the discussion, and formulate thoughtful responses. In negotiations or debates, strategic pauses can underscore a point's significance, allowing the gravity of words to sink in, or can be used to control the pace of conversation, guiding it towards a more reflective and meaningful exchange.

- Strategic deployment: Use silence to emphasize crucial points, allowing your words to resonate more deeply with the listener.

- Regulating conversation flow: Intentional pauses can slow down rapid exchanges, preventing escalation and facilitating a more measured, considerate dialogue.

Interpreting Silence

Understanding the nuanced meanings silence can convey requires keen observation and contextual awareness. Silence can signify contemplation, agreement, resistance, or emotional overwhelm, among other things. The key to navigating its varied interpretations lies in considering the broader context of the conversation, the relationship between the participants, and accompanying nonverbal cues. A pause in a heated debate might indicate a participant's attempt to calm rising emotions, while in a brainstorming session, it could signal deep engagement with the ideas presented.

- Contextual awareness: Evaluate the setting and dynamics of the conversation to accurately interpret the silence.

- Complementary cues: Look for nonverbal signals that accompany silence, such as body language or facial expressions, to gain insight into its underlying message.

The Power of Pausing

Incorporating pauses into speech is not merely a tactic; it's an acknowledgment of the listener's need to digest and engage with the information being shared. This practice can enhance clarity, improve comprehension, and foster a more interactive dialogue. Pauses offer a moment of respite for the speaker and listener alike, creating a rhythm that can make complex or dense information more accessible. Moreover, in moments of disagreement or tension, a well-timed pause can serve as a circuit breaker, providing an opportunity for emotions to settle and opening a pathway to constructive resolution.

- Enhancing comprehension: Use pauses to break information into manageable chunks, aiding the listener's understanding.

- Emotional regulation: Employ strategic pauses during discussions charged with strong emotions to allow for cooling off and reflection.

Practicing Silence

Becoming comfortable with silence and learning to wield it effectively within communication is a skill that can be cultivated through purposeful practice. The discomfort many feel in the face of silence often leads to its hasty filling, with words that may be unnecessary or counterproductive. To harness the full potential of silence, consider the following exercises:

- Silent observation: Spend periods in silent observation of your environment, attuning yourself to nonverbal cues and the unspoken elements of your surroundings. This practice can heighten your sensitivity to the communicative power of silence.

- Mindful listening: Engage in conversations where you consciously focus on listening, using silence as a tool to deepen your understanding of the speaker's message. Resist the urge to fill pauses immediately, instead allowing them to unfold naturally.

- Reflection periods: After speaking, institute brief periods of silence to reflect on what has been said before continuing. This can encourage more thoughtful and deliberate communication.

- Silence in solitude: Spend time in solitude, free from digital distractions, to become more comfortable with your own company and thoughts. This comfort with personal silence translates into ease with silence in conversation.

In the intricate dance of dialogue, silence emerges not as a gap but as a bridge, connecting words and worlds with its potent, unspoken language. Its strategic use can transform conversations, turning exchanges of information into opportunities for connection, reflection, and discovery. By understanding the multifaceted role of silence, interpreting its messages with care, and embracing the pause, we unlock new dimensions in our communication, enriching our interactions with depth and authenticity. In this light, silence is not merely the absence of sound but a profound presence, a vital component of the symphony of human communication.

Cultivating Patience: A Virtue in Listening

In the realm of communication, patience is not merely a virtue but a foundational pillar that underpins the edifice of effective listening. The capacity to remain patient, to afford space and time for thoughts to unfurl and words to find their path, enhances our ability to engage deeply and attentively with the speaker. This section delves into the symbiotic relationship between patience and listening, explores the modern-day challenges to nurturing patience, and offers strategies to cultivate this essential trait, ultimately underscoring how patience can influence and improve business outcomes.

The Link Between Patience and Effective Listening

At its heart, patience in listening is about allowing conversations to breathe, providing the speaker with the time needed to express themselves fully without rushing to conclusions or interjections. This practice not only affirms the speaker's value, making them feel heard and respected but also enriches the listener's understanding, as patience opens the door to nuances and insights that might otherwise be missed in haste.

- Enriched understanding: By embracing patience, listeners can capture the full spectrum of the message, including subtle nuances that are often overlooked in rapid exchanges.

- Affirmation of value: When listeners exhibit patience, speakers feel a sense of respect and worth, fostering an environment of trust and open communication.

Challenges to Patience in Fast-Paced Environments

The brisk pace of modern business environments often stands in stark contrast to the slow, deliberate nature of patient listening. In a world where speed is equated with efficiency and productivity, patience can erroneously be viewed as a hindrance, leading to a culture of rapid responses and half-heard messages. The challenge lies in resisting the urge to rush, to interrupt, and to respond without fully engaging with the speaker's message.

- Cultural emphasis on speed: The prevailing belief that faster is better can create pressure to respond quickly, at the expense of comprehensive understanding.

- Technological distractions: The constant barrage of notifications and the lure of multitasking can fragment attention, making patient listening all the more difficult.

Strategies for Developing Patience

Cultivating patience, especially in listening, requires intentional practice and a shift in perspective. It's about retraining our responses to align more closely with the principles of thoughtful engagement and reflective understanding.

- Mindfulness practices: Incorporating mindfulness into daily routines can enhance present-moment awareness, reducing the impulse to rush through conversations.

- Setting realistic expectations: Adjusting expectations about the time and attention required for meaningful conversations can help mitigate frustration and foster a more patient outlook.

- Active engagement techniques: Techniques such as note-taking or summarizing the speaker's points in your own words can anchor attention, making it easier to maintain patience.

The Impact of Patience on Business Outcomes

The cultivation of patience in listening is not merely a personal virtue but a strategic business asset. In leadership, negotiations, and team dynamics, patience can lead to more informed decision-making, stronger relationships, and a culture of respect and understanding.

- Informed decision-making: Patience affords the time to gather comprehensive information and consider multiple perspectives, leading to more nuanced and effective decisions.

- Stronger relationships: Demonstrating patience in listening signals respect and value, laying the foundation for lasting professional relationships built on mutual trust.

- Enhanced team dynamics: A culture that values patient listening encourages open communication, where ideas are fully explored and individuals feel genuinely heard.

In the intricate dance of communication, where words and silence play equal roles, patience emerges as a guiding light, illuminating the path to deeper understanding and connection. By fostering patience, we not only enhance our capacity to listen and comprehend but also elevate the quality of our interactions, leading to outcomes that are enriched by the depth and breadth of shared insights. In this way, patience transcends its role as a mere virtue, becoming a cornerstone of effective communication and a catalyst for success in the fast-paced world of business.

Transformative Listening: Changing Perspectives and Outcomes

Transformative listening steps beyond the traditional boundaries of hearing and responding to enter a realm where the primary goal is to understand and empathize. This mode of listening is not about seeking solutions or preparing to reply but about allowing the speaker's message to influence and potentially alter the listener's perspective. It's a deeply human approach to communication that recognizes the value in every word and silence, aiming to foster a connection that transcends mere transactional exchanges.

Defining Transformative Listening

Transformative listening is characterized by its focus on the speaker's underlying message, emotions, and intentions. It involves a willingness to be influenced by what is heard, to allow one's own views and understandings to be challenged and enriched by the perspectives of others. This form of listening requires a departure from the conventional focus on response and solution, emphasizing instead the value of presence, openness, and empathy in communication.

- Presence: Fully engaging with the speaker, without distraction.

- Openness: Being receptive to new ideas and perspectives, even when they challenge existing beliefs.

- Empathy: Striving to understand the speaker's emotional experience and viewpoint.

The Impact of Transformative Listening

The effects of transformative listening can be profound, both for individuals and organizations. By fostering an environment where every voice is not only heard but truly listened to, it becomes possible to resolve conflicts more effectively, spur innovation, and strengthen relationships. Transformative listening can shift perspectives, revealing common ground and new possibilities that were previously obscured by misunderstanding or disagreement.

- Conflict Resolution: By focusing on understanding rather than winning, transformative listening facilitates the discovery of mutually acceptable solutions.

- Fostering Innovation: Openness to diverse perspectives can spark creativity, leading to innovative solutions and approaches.

- Strengthening Relationships: Demonstrating genuine interest and empathy in listening can build trust and deepen connections.

Techniques for Practicing Transformative Listening

Cultivating the ability to engage in transformative listening involves developing specific skills and adopting a mindset geared toward openness and empathy. Some techniques to enhance transformative listening include:

- Suspending Judgment: Temporarily setting aside one's judgments and preconceptions to fully engage with the speaker's message.

- Reflective Mirroring: Rephrasing or summarizing what the speaker has said to confirm understanding and demonstrate empathy.

- Asking Open-Ended Questions: Encouraging the speaker to elaborate on their thoughts and feelings, can provide deeper insights and foster greater connection.

Examples of Transformative Listening in Action

Real-world examples highlight the power of transformative listening to effect positive change. In one corporate scenario, a series of misunderstandings between departments led to a breakdown in communication and collaboration. By initiating a series of dialogues centred on transformative listening, team members began to understand the challenges and pressures faced by their colleagues, leading to a renewed spirit of cooperation and a more cohesive approach to problem-solving.

Another example involves a manager who, through transformative listening, was able to detect the early signs of burnout in a high-performing employee. By genuinely understanding the employee's experience and concerns, the manager was able to implement changes that not only addressed the immediate issue but also led to improvements in team workload management and work-life balance.

These instances underscore how transformative listening can lead to significant positive changes, both in resolving immediate challenges and in fostering an atmosphere of mutual respect and collaboration.

As we consider the dynamics of effective communication, it becomes clear that the act of listening—truly listening—holds the key to unlocking deeper understanding and connection. Transformative listening, with its emphasis on empathy, openness, and the willingness to be influenced, represents a powerful tool for changing perspectives and outcomes. It encourages us to look beyond the surface of spoken words to the rich tapestry of meaning and emotion that lies beneath and to allow ourselves to be transformed by the experience of truly connecting with another.

In the broader context of communication, the practice of transformative listening serves as a reminder of the profound impact our approach to listening can have on our relationships, our workplaces, and our communities. It challenges us to listen not just with the intention of replying but with the intent to understand, empathize, and, ultimately, grow. As we move forward, let us carry with us the lessons of transformative listening, applying them not only in our conversations but in every aspect of our interactions with others.

From the Author:

I want you to meet Sarah. She was struggling to communicate effectively at work and home. While scrolling through Amazon she stumbled upon this one particular book, and read this one review that changed everything for her. How good would that feeling be if that review she read was yours and it changed her life forever?

Are you loving what you're reading so far? If you would like to help impact others like Sarah, I ask that you share your thoughts in a review. Your words could be the nudge someone needs.

You can leave a review by heading to where you got the book search for my book and scroll to **"Write a Review"** Share your thoughts on how the book has influenced your communication skills then hit the submit button to share your review

Thank you for making a difference

Chapter Four

The Unspoken Elements of Persuasion

Picture a silent film without a single word, emotions ripple, intentions clear, and stories unfold. This is the power of nonverbal communication. In the high-stakes world of business, where every handshake and glance can signify more than words ever could, understanding this silent language becomes critical. It's not just about what you say but how you say it and, more importantly, what you don't say at all. This chapter delves into the nuances of body language in business settings, offering insights into reading, interpreting, and leveraging nonverbal cues to enhance communication and negotiation outcomes.

The Vocabulary of Body Language

Body language speaks volumes in any interaction, especially in business. It includes posture, gestures, facial expressions, and even the distance one keeps. Each movement, or lack thereof, can communicate confidence, anxiety, openness, or resistance. Recognizing the 'vocabulary' of body language and its significance can transform interactions, making them more productive and meaningful.

- Posture can suggest confidence or discomfort. Standing or sitting straight, with shoulders back, typically conveys assurance.

- Gestures, like nodding, can show agreement or understanding, while crossed arms might suggest defensiveness.

- Facial expressions offer a window into a person's emotional state. A genuine smile fosters trust, while a furrowed brow might indicate confusion or concern.

- Proximity and personal space vary culturally but can indicate how comfortable people are with each other or the conversation.

Reading Body Language Accurately

Interpreting body language correctly requires attention and practice. Misreading cues can lead to misunderstandings or missed opportunities. Here are some tips for accurate interpretation:

- Observe in clusters. A single gesture or expression might be misleading; look for consistent patterns.

- Context matters. Consider the situation and the individual's normal behavior as a baseline.

- Nonverbal cues complement verbal communication. They can affirm or contradict what's being said, providing deeper insight into the message.

Misinterpretations and Cultural Differences

Misinterpretation of body language can lead to awkward situations or communication breakdowns. Awareness of cultural differences is crucial, as gestures and expressions can have varying meanings across cultures. For instance, direct eye contact considered assertive and trustworthy in some Western cultures might be perceived as disrespectful in some Asian cultures.

- Research and ask questions about cultural norms when interacting with international colleagues or clients.

- Stay observant and adaptable. If you notice discomfort or confusion, adjust your behaviour accordingly.

- When in doubt, default to more neutral expressions and gestures.

Applying Body Language Insights

Leveraging your understanding of body language can enhance communication and negotiation outcomes. It allows you to adjust your approach based on the nonverbal feedback you receive, building stronger connections and fostering mutual understanding.

- Mirror the body language of your conversation partner to create rapport and ease.

- Use open gestures and maintain appropriate eye contact to convey sincerity and confidence.

- Be mindful of your own body language. Ensure it aligns with your message and the impression you want to make.

Exercises for Practicing Body Language Awareness

1. Observation Exercise: Spend a day observing the body language of people around you, noting gestures, postures, and expressions. Reflect on what these nonverbal cues communicated to you.

2. Feedback Session: In a comfortable setting with a colleague or friend, discuss a topic and ask for feedback on your body language. Were your gestures and expressions congruent with your words?

3. Role-play Scenarios: Practice business interactions with a partner, focusing on nonverbal communication. Afterward, share insights on what was communicated nonverbally.

Reflection Section

After completing the exercises, reflect on the following questions:

- Were there any surprises in how your body language was perceived by others?

- How did your perception of others' nonverbal cues change after the observation exercise?

- What adjustments can you make to ensure your body language aligns more closely with your intended message?

Resource List

For further exploration of body language in business contexts, the following resources are recommended:

- "The Definitive Book of Body Language" by Allan and Barbara Pease offers comprehensive insights into reading and interpreting body language.

- "What Every BODY is Saying" by Joe Navarro provides a former FBI agent's perspective on using body language for advantage in negotiations.

- Online courses on nonverbal communication can also provide interactive learning experiences to enhance your understanding and application of body language insights.

Understanding and applying the nuances of body language can significantly impact your effectiveness in business communication. Whether it's securing a deal, leading a team, or navigating a networking event, your nonverbal cues play a crucial role in shaping outcomes. Armed with the insights from this chapter, you're better equipped to read the unspoken signals in your next business interaction, leveraging the silent elements of persuasion to your advantage.

The Impact of Eye Contact on Trust and Persuasion

Eye contact, one of the most potent nonverbal cues, operates silently but significantly in the realm of business communication. Its power to bridge gaps and forge connections cannot be overstated. When two parties lock gazes, even briefly, a channel of trust and understanding is established, paving the way for more open and effective exchanges. This section will explore the multifaceted role of eye contact in business interactions, emphasizing its influence on trust, the necessity for balance, cultural considerations, and methods to enhance eye contact skills for better business outcomes.

Eye Contact and Connection

The act of making eye contact serves as a nonverbal handshake, an unspoken agreement to engage and connect. It signals interest, attentiveness, and respect, laying a foundation for trust. When someone meets your gaze, it's as if they're affirming, "I see you, I acknowledge your presence, and I am open to this interaction." This mutual recognition is crucial in business settings where trust is the currency of successful relationships. Whether pitching to potential investors, leading a team meeting, or negotiating with a client, maintaining appropriate eye contact can significantly reinforce your message's sincerity and credibility.

- It fosters a sense of mutual respect and openness, encouraging more honest and productive conversations.
- Signals attentiveness, showing that you are fully engaged and value the interaction and the person you are communicating with.

Balancing Eye Contact

While eye contact is undeniably powerful, its impact largely depends on finding the right balance. Too little, and you risk appearing disinterested or evasive; too much, and you may seem overly aggressive or confrontational. The key is to maintain eye contact that feels natural and comfortable for both parties. This balance not only varies from one individual to another but also shifts according to the context of the interaction.

- Aim for a balanced approach, where sustained eye contact is interspersed with natural breaks, to avoid overwhelming the other person.
- Observing the other party's response to your gaze can guide you in adjusting your eye contact to maintain comfort and connection.

Cultural Nuances in Eye Contact

Eye contact is not a universal language; its interpretations vary dramatically across cultures. In some Western cultures, for instance, firm eye contact is associated with confidence and honesty. In contrast, in many Asian cultures, prolonged eye contact may be perceived as disrespectful or confrontational. Navigating these cultural nuances is vital for global business professionals who must communicate effectively across diverse cultural landscapes.

- Before international interactions, research the eye contact norms of the other party's culture to avoid misunderstandings.

- When unsure, adopting a moderate level of eye contact is generally a safe strategy, allowing you to adjust based on the other person's cues.

Practical Exercises for Eye Contact

Improving your eye contact skills can significantly enhance your communication and persuasion capabilities in business settings. Here are some exercises designed to refine your ability to use eye contact effectively:

1. Eye Contact Drills: Pair up with a colleague or friend and engage in a conversation while consciously maintaining eye contact. Start with short intervals, gradually increasing the duration as you become more comfortable.

2. Recording and Review: Record yourself delivering a presentation or pitch. Review the recording, noting your use of eye contact. Identify moments where more or less eye contact could have improved the impact of your message.

3. Mirror Practice: Stand in front of a mirror and speak about a topic you're passionate about. Maintain eye contact with your reflection, observing how your gaze accompanies the flow of your speech. This exercise helps in becoming more conscious of your natural eye contact patterns.

4. Observation in Public Spaces: Sit in a public area and observe interactions around you. Take note of how people use eye contact in various contexts – greeting, conversing, or negotiating. Reflect on how the use or avoidance of eye contact affects your perception of these interactions.

Through these practices, you can develop a more nuanced understanding and control of your eye contact, enabling you to use it more strategically in your business communications. Whether you're looking to build trust, convey confidence, or navigate cultural differences, mastering the art of eye contact can open doors to more meaningful and persuasive interactions in the business world.

Posture and Presence: Conveying Confidence Without Words

In the nuanced theatre of business communication, posture and presence serve as silent narrators of one's story, subtly conveying confidence, openness, or defensiveness without uttering a single word. This section unravels the intricate dance of nonverbal cues, guiding you on how to harness your physical stance and aura to make a powerful statement in any business scenario.

The Language of Posture

The way you hold yourself speaks volumes before you even begin to verbalize your thoughts. A slouched posture may inadvertently signal disinterest or lack of confidence, while an upright stance can project strength and readiness. This nonverbal language of posture plays a crucial role in first impressions and ongoing interactions, influencing how you are perceived and how effectively you can command attention and respect.

- Confidence: An upright posture, with shoulders back and head held high, communicates self-assurance and poise.
- Openness: Keeping your arms uncrossed and hands visible suggests you are open to dialogue and collaboration.
- Defensiveness: Crossed arms or a closed stance could be interpreted as resistance or discomfort, potentially putting others on guard.

Adjusting Posture for Impact

Navigating different business settings demands adaptability in how you present yourself physically. The boardroom, a networking event, and a casual team meeting each call for a nuanced approach to posture that aligns with the context and desired outcome of the interaction.

- In formal presentations, stand firmly with an open stance to exude confidence and command attention.
- During negotiations, adopting a slightly leaning forward position

can signify engagement and interest in finding common ground.

- In collaborative settings, mirroring the posture of your counterparts can foster rapport and cooperation.

The Role of Presence in Communication

Beyond posture, the concept of 'presence'—the ability to command attention and convey authority through one's demeanour—plays a pivotal role in effective communication and leadership. Presence is the invisible yet palpable force that makes people take notice and listen intently, turning ordinary interactions into impactful experiences. It is cultivated through a combination of confidence, authenticity, and the ability to be fully engaged in the moment.

- **Confidence and authenticity:** Projecting an aura of self-assurance, grounded in genuine self-awareness and understanding of one's strengths and weaknesses.
- **Engagement:** Showing a deep interest in the conversation and the people involved, making them feel seen and heard.

Exercises for Improving Posture and Presence

Developing a commanding presence and an impactful posture is a journey of self-awareness and continuous practice. Here are exercises designed to enhance your nonverbal communication skills, helping you to stand out in any business setting.

1. Daily Posture Check-ins: Set reminders throughout the day to assess and adjust your posture. Are your shoulders slouched? Is your back not straight? Correcting your posture regularly can help develop muscle memory for a more natural, confident stance.

2. Power Pose Practice: Before important meetings or presentations, spend a few minutes in a 'power pose'—standing in a posture of confidence, such as hands on hips or arms raised in victory. This exercise, based on social psychology research, can boost feelings of confidence and presence.

3. Mindful Walking: Practice walking with purpose and poise. Focus on maintaining an upright posture, making eye contact, and acknowledging others with a nod or smile. This practice can enhance your presence in motion, making your arrivals and departures memorable.

4. Video Feedback Sessions: Record yourself during practice presentations or conversations. Review the recordings to observe your posture, presence, and engagement level. Note areas for improvement and track your progress over time.

By integrating these practices into your routine, you can refine your posture and presence, transforming them into powerful tools in your communication arsenal. Whether you are leading a team, pitching to clients, or networking with peers, your nonverbal cues can set the tone for successful interactions, paving the way for meaningful connections and opportunities. Through mindful attention to how you present yourself physically and energetically, you can elevate your impact in the business world, moving beyond words to communicate with confidence and authority.

The Subtleties of Spatial Dynamics in Communication

In the nuanced arena of business communication, the silent dance of spatial dynamics plays a pivotal role, often overlooked yet fundamental in shaping interactions and outcomes. This section sheds light on the intricate ways space influences communication, from personal boundaries to cross-cultural perceptions, and offers strategies for effectively navigating and leveraging spatial dynamics to enhance communication in various business contexts.

Understanding Personal Space

At the heart of spatial dynamics lies the concept of personal space, an invisible bubble that surrounds us, its size fluctuating based on context, culture, and individual preference. In business interactions, respecting personal space is crucial; it communicates respect and consideration, fostering a comfortable environment conducive to open dialogue. Violating this unspoken boundary can lead to discomfort, creating barriers to effective communication.

- Personal space varies among individuals; some may prefer close interactions, while others need more distance.

- Observing and respecting these preferences is key to maintaining comfort and trust in professional relationships.

Spatial Dynamics in Different Cultures

The perception of space and its use in communication varies widely across cultures, influencing interactions in the global business landscape. In some cultures, close proximity and physical touch during conversation are norms, signalling warmth and trust. In contrast, other cultures value a larger personal bubble, viewing too close an approach as intrusive. Understanding these cultural nuances is critical for international business professionals seeking to communicate effectively and build relationships across borders.

- In high-context cultures, such as those in East Asia and the Middle East, closer distances and more frequent touches might be common during interactions.

- Low-context cultures, typical of North American and Northern European countries, often maintain larger personal spaces and minimal physical contact.

- Adapting to the spatial norms of different cultures can significantly improve communication effectiveness and foster mutual respect.

Using Space to Enhance Communication

Strategically managing spatial dynamics can amplify the impact of communication, particularly in meetings and negotiations. The arrangement of a room, the positioning of chairs, and even where you choose to stand can subtly influence the flow and tone of the conversation. By consciously considering these elements, you can create an environment that promotes engagement, collaboration, and positive outcomes.

- Positioning yourself at an equal distance from all participants during a meeting can facilitate a sense of equality and encourage open participation.

- In negotiations, sitting side by side with the other party, rather than directly across, can reduce feelings of confrontation, making it easier to reach mutual agreements.

- Adjusting the layout of a room to remove barriers, such as large tables, can foster a more intimate and cooperative atmosphere.

Navigating Space in Collaborative Environments

Open-plan workspaces and collaborative environments present unique challenges and opportunities in managing spatial dynamics. While designed to foster teamwork and fluid communication, these settings can sometimes lead to overcrowding and sensory overload, hindering effective interaction. Navigating these spaces requires a delicate balance of accessibility and boundary-setting to ensure productive communication.

- Establishing clear norms around personal space and privacy can help maintain comfort and respect among team members.

- Creating designated quiet zones or privacy areas within open workspaces can provide necessary retreats for focused work or sensitive conversations.

- Encouraging the use of nonverbal cues, such as headphones to signal 'do not disturb' or flags to indicate availability, can help manage interruptions and foster respectful engagement.

In the intricate ballet of business communication, spatial dynamics emerge as a silent yet powerful force, shaping perceptions, influencing interactions, and ultimately affecting outcomes. By gaining a deeper understanding of personal space, recognizing and adapting to cultural variations in spatial norms, and strategically employing space to enhance communication, professionals can navigate the complexities of the modern business environment with greater finesse and effectiveness. Whether in the boardroom, at a networking event, or within the collaborative buzz of an open-plan office, mastering the subtleties of spatial dynamics can unlock new dimensions of connection and success in the business world.

Using Gestures to Enhance Your Message

In the theatre of professional discourse, the silent chorus of gestures plays a significant role, amplifying the impact of spoken words. These physical movements, when aligned with verbal communication, can add a layer of emphasis, clarity, and emotion, enriching the narrative being conveyed. This segment explores the multifaceted nature of gestures, their interpretations across different scenarios, identifies those that may hinder rather than help, and provides guidance on developing a repertoire of gestures that enhance rather than detract from your message.

The Power of Gestures

Gestures encompass a wide range of physical movements, from the subtle nod of agreement to the expansive arm gestures that accompany a passionate plea. They serve as visual cues that can strengthen the message, evoke emotions, and assist in the retention of information. When speaking, the incorporation of appropriate gestures can make the narrative more engaging, helping to draw the listener in and hold their attention.

- Gestures can underscore key points, making them more memorable.
- They help break down complex information into understandable chunks, aiding comprehension.
- Through gestures, speakers can convey enthusiasm and conviction, making the message more persuasive.

Types of Gestures and Their Meanings

Gestures can be broadly categorized into several types, each carrying distinct meanings and used in various contexts to communicate specific messages.

- Illustrators: These gestures are directly tied to the spoken word, such as using fingers to enumerate points or miming shapes to describe objects. They clarify and augment verbal messages.

- **Emblems:** These are culturally specific gestures with well-defined meanings, independent of speech, such as the thumbs up for approval or a nod for 'yes'. Their interpretation varies significantly around the globe.

- **Regulators:** These control the flow of conversation, for instance, raising a hand to signal a desire to speak or nodding to encourage the speaker to continue.

- **Adaptors:** Often subconscious, these gestures reflect internal feelings or manage discomfort, like tapping a pen when anxious or adjusting a tie for self-assurance.

Gestures to Avoid

While gestures can significantly enhance communication, certain movements may be misinterpreted, distracting, or even offensive, particularly in a professional setting. Recognizing and avoiding these can prevent unintended messages from undermining your intended communication.

- **Pointing:** Using a finger to point can come across as aggressive or accusatory. Opt for an open-handed gesture to direct attention.

- **Fidgeting:** Repeated small movements, such as tapping feet or playing with hair, can signal nervousness or impatience, detracting from the speaker's credibility.

- **Crossed arms:** Often interpreted as a defensive stance, may create a barrier to open communication.

- **Excessive or repetitive gestures:** Overuse of any gesture can be distracting and may dilute the impact of the message.

Cultivating Effective Gesturing Habits

Developing a set of gestures that complements and enhances verbal communication requires awareness, practice, and feedback. Here are strategies to refine your gesturing habits:

- **Self-awareness:** Start by becoming conscious of your natural gesturing habits. Record yourself during presentations or meetings to identify your go-to gestures and any fidgeting behaviours.

- Moderation is key: Use gestures purposefully, ensuring they align with and emphasize your message. Avoid over-gesturing, which can overwhelm the audience.

- Practice: Rehearse your presentations or conversations, integrating gestures thoughtfully. This helps in making them feel more natural and less forced.

- Feedback: Seek input from trusted colleagues or mentors on your use of gestures. Constructive criticism can offer insights into how your gestures are perceived and areas for improvement.

By thoughtfully integrating gestures into your communication repertoire, you can significantly enhance the clarity, impact, and persuasiveness of your message. Gestures serve not just as embellishments to speech but as integral components of effective communication, capable of bridging gaps between words and meanings, enriching the narrative, and fostering a deeper connection with your audience. As with any aspect of communication, the key lies in balance and relevance, ensuring that your physical expressions align with and amplify your words, creating a cohesive and compelling narrative that resonates with your listeners.

The Power of Touch in Nonverbal Business Communication

In the intricate dance of professional interactions, the nuanced gesture of touch plays a pivotal role, often operating beneath the conscious level of communication yet profoundly impacting the dynamics of business relationships. Its capacity to convey a spectrum of messages, from support and reassurance to authority and dominance, underscores its significance in the nonverbal lexicon of business etiquette. This segment aims to unravel the complexities surrounding the use of touch in professional settings, navigating its potential with sensitivity and awareness to enhance, rather than complicate, business interactions.

The Role of Touch in Communication

Touch, in its essence, is a primary form of human connection, predating verbal language in our evolutionary history. Its use in communication is deeply ingrained, capable of conveying sentiments that words sometimes cannot. In the business realm, a firm handshake, a light pat on the back, or a gentle touch on the arm during a conversation can serve as powerful conveyors of solidarity, agreement, or empathy. However, the appropriateness of touch is heavily context-dependent, influenced by cultural norms, personal boundaries, and the nature of the relationship between the parties involved.

- A handshake remains the most universally accepted form of touch in business, symbolizing respect and goodwill.
- Congratulatory gestures, such as a brief pat on the back or shoulder, can express appreciation and foster a sense of team spirit, provided they are used judiciously and with mutual respect.

Appropriate Use of Touch in Business

Navigating the use of touch in professional settings demands a keen understanding of boundaries and an acute sensitivity to individual comfort levels. The golden rule is to lean towards the side of caution, recognizing that what may be intended as a gesture of support or camaraderie can be misinterpreted or unwelcome.

- Always observe the other person's body language for cues of receptiveness or discomfort and adjust your actions accordingly.
- Avoid potentially ambiguous gestures, such as hugs or touches that linger, which may be perceived as intrusive or inappropriate in a business context.

Touch and Nonverbal Cues

Touch does not exist in isolation but interacts dynamically with other nonverbal cues to shape the overall communication experience. Its impact is often amplified or modulated by accompanying facial expressions, posture, and tone of voice. For instance, a reassuring touch on the arm, coupled with a sincere smile and open posture, can significantly enhance a message of support and solidarity. Conversely, the same gesture, if accompanied by a closed posture or indifferent facial expression, may convey mixed signals, leading to confusion or discomfort.

- Synchronize your touch with positive facial expressions and open body language to reinforce the intended message.
- Be mindful of the congruence between verbal messages and nonverbal signals, including touch, to ensure clarity and coherence in communication.

Navigating Touch in a Global Business Context

In an increasingly globalized business world, understanding and respecting cultural differences in the use of touch is paramount. What constitutes acceptable touch varies widely across cultures – from the frequent use of touch in Mediterranean and Latin American cultures to the more reserved approaches in many Asian and Nordic cultures. Failure to appreciate these differences can lead to misunderstandings, inadvertently offending clients or colleagues from different cultural backgrounds.

- Before international interactions, research the touch norms of the respective culture to avoid faux pas. When in doubt, follow the lead of your international counterparts, allowing them to initiate any gestures of touch.
- In multicultural teams, fostering an environment of openness and dialogue about cultural preferences and boundaries can help navigate the complexities of touch and other nonverbal cues, ensuring that all team members feel respected and comfortable.

Touch, when used with awareness and sensitivity, can be a subtle yet powerful tool in enhancing communication, building relationships, and conveying leadership in the professional arena. Its capacity to transmit empathy, support, and respect can bridge gaps, fostering an environment of trust and mutual understanding. However, its potential to miscommunicate or transgress underscores the need for a mindful approach, attuned to the nuances of context, culture, and individual preference. In mastering the delicate art of touch within the tapestry of nonverbal business communication, professionals can unlock deeper levels of connection and collaboration, enriching their interactions and paving the way for more meaningful and effective business relationships.

Dress and Appearance: Silent Communicators of Professionalism

The moment you step into a room before a single word escapes your lips, your attire speaks volumes. It's a silent but potent communicator, setting the stage for first impressions and often determining the tone of the interactions that follow. In the world of business, where professionalism is paramount, understanding the language of dress and appearance is not just about adhering to a dress code but about strategically using your attire to convey the desired message and enhance your brand.

First Impressions and Attire

The adage "You never get a second chance to make a first impression" holds especially true when it comes to professional settings. Within seconds of meeting you, people form opinions based on your appearance. These judgments, though superficial, can significantly impact your ability to connect and communicate effectively. A well-tailored suit, for instance, can project authority and competence, making it an ideal choice for situations where you want to command respect, such as in negotiations or high-stakes meetings. Conversely, an outfit that is too casual or dishevelled can undermine your credibility, regardless of your skills or experience.

To ensure your attire contributes positively to first impressions, consider the expectations of your industry and aim for a look that is polished and professional yet authentic to your style.

Dressing for Different Business Contexts

Navigating the expectations of various business environments requires a versatile wardrobe and an understanding of the subtleties of professional attire. The appropriate dress code can vary widely, from the formal suits expected in traditional corporate settings to the smart casual or business casual attire more common in creative industries and startups.

- For formal meetings or presentations, opt for classic and conservative choices that emphasize professionalism.

- In more relaxed settings, such as casual networking events or company retreats, smart casual attire allows for comfort while still maintaining a professional image.

- When transitioning between different types of events in a single day, layering can offer flexibility, allowing you to adjust your outfit to suit the formality of each occasion.

The Psychology of Colour in Attire

Colour plays a crucial role in communication, with each hue capable of evoking specific emotions and perceptions. In the context of business attire, selecting colours strategically can enhance the impact of your appearance, influencing how others perceive and respond to you.

- Blue, often associated with trust, stability, and confidence, is a wise choice for interviews or client meetings where you want to establish credibility.

- Red, a colour linked to energy, passion, and action, can be a powerful accent for presentations or sales pitches, drawing attention and demonstrating enthusiasm.

- Neutral tones like grey, black, and white project professionalism and can serve as a versatile foundation for your wardrobe, allowing you to adapt to various settings and occasions with ease.

Personal Branding Through Appearance

Your attire and appearance are integral components of your brand, reflecting your professional identity and values. By consciously curating your wardrobe, you can craft an image that not only aligns with your career aspirations but also distinguishes you in a competitive field.

- Consistency is key to reinforcing your brand. Choose a signature style or colour palette that reflects your professional persona, making you instantly recognizable and memorable.

- Accessories, from watches and jewellery to bags and briefcases, offer opportunities to express individuality and attention to detail, enhancing your brand without compromising professionalism.

- Grooming should not be overlooked, as it complements your attire and completes your professional image. Regular haircuts, neat nails, and minimal, tasteful makeup can polish your appearance, making you appear more put-together and competent.

In the dynamic landscape of professional interactions, where nonverbal cues can significantly influence outcomes, dress and appearance emerge as silent yet eloquent messengers of your competence, credibility, and character. By mastering the subtle language of professional attire, you not only ensure that your first impression is a lasting one but also leverage your appearance as a powerful tool for communication and personal branding. Whether you're stepping into a boardroom, presenting at a conference, or networking with peers, your choice of attire is a strategic decision, one that can open doors, build connections, and pave the way for success in the ever-evolving world of business.

The Role of Environment in Communication Efficacy

The spaces in which we communicate, whether physical or virtual, subtly influence the flow and effectiveness of our interactions. Just as a theatre stage is set to create an ambiance that enhances the audience's experience, so too can the environments in which business communications occur be optimized to support clarity, understanding, and engagement. This section explores how environmental factors impact communication and offers guidance on creating settings that promote effective exchanges.

Environmental factors in communication

The surroundings in which dialogue takes place can significantly impact the participants' ability to express themselves clearly, listen actively, and engage fully. Elements such as lighting, noise levels, and the overall layout contribute to the ambiance of a space, each with the potential to either facilitate or hinder the communication process.

- Lighting sets the tone of the interaction; too dim, and it can induce a sense of lethargy or strain, too bright, and it may cause discomfort or distraction.

- Noise levels must be managed carefully. Excessive background noise can obscure verbal communication and disrupt concentration, while a completely silent space might feel overly formal or intimidating, stifling open dialogue.

- Layout influences how participants interact within a space. An arrangement that places barriers between individuals can impede the free flow of conversation, whereas a more open setup encourages inclusivity and exchange.

Designing spaces for effective communication

Creating environments that enhance communication involves thoughtful consideration of the intended use and the participant's needs. For meetings and negotiations, the goal is to foster an atmosphere of collaboration and respect, where ideas can be exchanged freely and without undue influence from the setting itself.

- Choose a neutral space that does not confer an advantage to any party, ensuring all participants feel equally comfortable and empowered to contribute.

- Arrange seating to facilitate eye contact and engagement among participants, using a round table or a semi-circle layout to avoid hierarchies.

- Minimize distractions by selecting a location away from high-traffic areas and ensuring the space is free from unnecessary digital interruptions.

Virtual environments and communication

As the business world increasingly embraces remote and hybrid models, the virtual environments in which we communicate have come under scrutiny for their impact on the efficacy of exchanges. The design and management of these digital spaces are critical to overcoming the inherent challenges of distance and technology.

- In video conferences, encourage participants to use backgrounds that minimize distraction and convey professionalism, whether through neutral real environments or subtle digital backdrops.

- Optimize audio and visual settings to ensure all participants can be seen and heard clearly, using high-quality microphones and cameras as needed.

- Facilitate engagement by making use of features like hand-raising to manage turn-taking, chat functions for sharing ideas without interrupting, and break-out rooms for smaller group discussions.

Adapting to environmental challenges

Even with careful planning, environmental challenges can arise, threatening to disrupt communication. Being prepared to identify and address these issues promptly ensures that the focus remains on the interaction rather than the setting.

- Should noise become an issue, be ready to move to a quieter location if possible, or use technology like noise-cancelling microphones to mitigate the impact.

- If a physical meeting space feels too formal or confrontational for the discussion at hand, suggest a walking meeting outdoors, where movement and a change of scenery can inspire more relaxed and creative dialogue.

- In virtual meetings, if participants experience connectivity issues, have a plan in place for quickly reestablishing links, such as switching to audio-only mode to conserve bandwidth or having backup communication channels ready.

The environments in which we communicate play a foundational role in the success of our interactions, shaping the dynamics of dialogue and influencing the outcomes of our exchanges. By giving due consideration to the setting, whether physical or digital, and making conscious choices to enhance the space for communication, we can significantly improve the clarity, effectiveness, and satisfaction of our professional interactions. It is through this attention to detail and adaptability to challenges that we can create environments conducive to meaningful dialogue and collaboration, fostering a culture of open, effective communication that drives progress and innovation.

Nonverbal Cues in Virtual Meetings: Navigating the New Normal

In the landscape of modern business communication, virtual meetings have swiftly transitioned from a convenience to a cornerstone. This shift has necessitated a re-evaluation of nonverbal cues, those silent yet impactful signals we rely on to convey and interpret messages beyond words. The digital realm presents unique challenges and opportunities in this regard, compelling us to adapt our strategies to maintain the subtlety and richness of face-to-face interactions.

Adapting Nonverbal Cues for Virtual Settings

The transition to screen-based communication strips away the physical context that enriches interaction, pressing us to find new ways to express and read nonverbal signals. In virtual meetings, our repertoire of gestures, facial expressions, and eye contact must be recalibrated to fit within the confines of a webcam's field of view.

- Gestures become more deliberate in a virtual format. A thumbs-up or a nod must be more pronounced to be noticed, given the limitations of screen size and video quality.

- Facial expressions play a heightened role due to the focus on the face within the video frame. Smiles, frowns, and nods need to be slightly exaggerated to ensure they are communicated effectively across digital mediums.

- Eye contact in virtual settings involves looking directly at the camera rather than the on-screen images of participants. This creates the illusion of direct eye contact, fostering a sense of connection and engagement.

EFFECTIVE COMMUNICATION SKILLS

Enhancing Virtual Presence

The concept of presence in virtual meetings extends beyond simply being seen or heard; it's about making your participation felt. Achieving this requires attention to several key factors that influence your virtual visibility and engagement.

- Camera angles and positioning: Position your camera at eye level to mimic the effect of sitting across from meeting participants. This setup encourages more natural interactions and helps maintain engagement.
- Lighting: Ensure your face is well-lit, preferably with natural light or a soft artificial source placed in front of you. Proper lighting can significantly improve how you are perceived and reduce misinterpretation of facial expressions.
- Background: Opt for a simple, uncluttered background that minimizes distractions. Virtual backgrounds can be used judiciously to maintain professionalism and reduce visual noise.

Reading Nonverbal Cues Online

The subtleties of nonverbal communication can be harder to discern in virtual meetings, necessitating a keen eye and heightened sensitivity to pick up on cues that might otherwise go unnoticed.

- Micro-expressions: Pay close attention to the brief, involuntary facial expressions that flit across participants' faces. These can provide valuable insights into their reactions and feelings.
- Posture and movement: Observing how individuals position themselves in front of the camera, along with any movements or shifts, can offer clues about their level of interest and engagement.
- Participation patterns: Note who speaks up, who leans in, and who remains passive. These behaviours can indicate levels of confidence, agreement, or reluctance that are not explicitly voiced.

Challenges and Solutions

Despite our best efforts, conveying and interpreting nonverbal cues in virtual settings is fraught with challenges. Yet, for every obstacle, there are practical solutions that can enhance the quality and effectiveness of digital communication.

- Limited field of view: Encourage participants to use their hands and faces expressively within the camera frame to convey enthusiasm, agreement, or questioning.

- Technical issues: Audio lags or freezes can disrupt the flow of nonverbal communication. Encourage attendees to use the chat function to express agreement or share quick thoughts when technical issues arise.

- Participant distraction: To minimize multitasking, employ engagement strategies such as regular check-ins, polls, or directed questions to keep attendees focused and active in the discussion.

- Cultural differences: When working with international teams, allocate time for participants to share their comfort levels and preferences regarding camera use, participation, and interpretation of nonverbal cues, fostering a more inclusive and respectful virtual environment.

In the realm of virtual meetings, where the traditional nuances of face-to-face interaction are diluted by screens and miles, our approach to nonverbal communication must evolve. By consciously adapting our gestures, refining our virtual presence, becoming adept at reading digital nonverbal cues, and navigating the inherent challenges with practical solutions, we can preserve the depth and richness of our interactions. In doing so, we not only overcome the barriers posed by distance and technology but also harness the potential of virtual platforms to forge connections that are as meaningful and impactful as those we build in person.

Cross-Cultural Nonverbal Communication: Navigating Global Business

EFFECTIVE COMMUNICATION SKILLS

In the global arena of business, the subtleties of nonverbal communication extend beyond personal quirks or organizational culture, deeply rooted in the rich soils of national and ethnic traditions. Understanding these variances is not just about avoiding faux pas; it's about building bridges without words, where mutual respect and understanding lay the pavement for successful international collaborations.

Nonverbal cues, from the distance we keep during a conversation to the way we express agreement or dissent, can vary dramatically across cultures. For instance, the firmness of a handshake, viewed as a sign of confidence in numerous Western cultures, might not be as emphasized in certain Asian cultures where it could be perceived as aggressive. Similarly, the direct eye contact that's valued in North American business settings could be seen as disrespectful in some Asian countries, where averting one's gaze is a sign of respect.

Cultural differences in nonverbal communication

The landscape of global business requires a nuanced understanding of these cultural differences. For example, in Japan, a bow has nuances of meaning depending on the angle and duration, expressing everything from a casual greeting to deep respect or apology. In contrast, Middle Eastern cultures value close physical proximity and touch among the same genders during conversations, a practice that might be uncomfortable for those from more reserved cultures.

Case studies of cross-cultural communication

Illustrating the importance of cultural sensitivity, a case study involving a UK-based firm and its new branch in Japan highlights the potential for misunderstanding. The British executives' habit of slapping backs and making direct eye contact was initially perceived as overly familiar and somewhat rude by their Japanese counterparts. Recognizing this, the company initiated cross-cultural workshops. These sessions helped both sides appreciate the nuances of their differing nonverbal cues, facilitating smoother communication and stronger relationships.

Another example involves an American tech company negotiating with a Brazilian firm. The Americans misinterpreted their Brazilian counterparts' frequent interruptions as rudeness, not realizing that in Brazilian culture, such interruptions are a sign of engagement and interest. Through open dialogue and cultural exchange, both parties learned to interpret each other's communication styles more accurately, leading to a successful partnership.

Strategies for cross-cultural competence

Developing competence in cross-cultural nonverbal communication involves several key strategies:

- Education and Awareness: Proactively learn about the cultures you interact with including their nonverbal communication norms. This knowledge can prevent misunderstandings and show respect for your international colleagues and partners.

- Observation and Adaptation: Pay close attention to the nonverbal cues used by your international counterparts. Be willing to adapt your behaviour to align more closely with their cultural norms, showing respect and flexibility.

- Seek Clarification: When in doubt, politely ask for clarification to avoid misinterpretation. This can also serve as an opportunity for cultural exchange and learning.

Navigating misinterpretations

Misinterpretations of nonverbal cues in cross-cultural interactions are not uncommon but can be navigated with patience and understanding. When faced with a potential misunderstanding, address it directly and with sensitivity. Express your intent clearly and inquire about the preferred norms, demonstrating your respect for cultural differences and your commitment to effective communication.

For instance, if you notice a colleague from a different culture seems uncomfortable with the physical proximity during a conversation, consider respectfully asking if they would prefer to have more space. This not only addresses the immediate discomfort but also opens a channel for dialogue about each other's preferences and norms, enriching the relationship with mutual understanding and respect.

In the woven fabric of global business, the threads of nonverbal communication add depth and colour, enhancing the tapestry of our interactions. By approaching these differences with curiosity, openness, and respect, we not only navigate the complexities of international business with more grace but also enrich our professional relationships and collaborations. The effort to understand and adapt to the nonverbal communication styles of different cultures not only smooths the path to business success but also contributes to a broader culture of respect and appreciation for diversity.

As we look beyond the nuances of nonverbal communication, our journey through the landscape of effective business interactions continues. The insights gained here lay the groundwork for deeper exploration and understanding, reminding us that communication, in all its forms, is the bedrock upon which successful business relationships are built.

Chapter Five

Navigating Digital Correspondence: The New Era of Professional Communication

In an age where a single email can bridge continents in seconds, the art of digital correspondence has never been more critical. This chapter peels back the layers of crafting emails that not only get opened but also acted upon, ensuring your message cuts through the digital noise of today's overflowing inboxes.

Email Etiquette: Crafting Messages That Get Read

Conciseness and Clarity

In the realm of digital communication, less is often more. With attention spans dwindling and inboxes bustling, your emails need to hit the sweet spot between brevity and substance. Think of your email as an elevator pitch: it must be short enough to maintain interest but comprehensive enough to convey the essential message. Start with a clear objective, use bullet points for easier digestion, and always conclude with a straightforward call to action. Remember, if you can't summarize the purpose of your email in one sentence, it might need refining.

The Art of Subject Lines

The subject line is your first, and sometimes only, chance to grab the reader's attention. It should act like a headline, compelling enough to pique interest while accurately reflecting the email's content. Experiment with including specifics such as dates, deadlines, or direct benefits to the reader. For instance, instead of "Meeting Request," try "Requesting Your Input: Marketing Strategy Meeting, Oct 10th." This approach not only catches the eye but also sets clear expectations for what the email entails.

Tone and Professionalism

Maintaining a professional tone doesn't mean your emails have to be devoid of personality. The key is to strike a balance that reflects respect for the recipient while also showcasing your unique voice. Avoid overly casual language, slang, or jargon that might not be universally understood. Instead, opt for clear, concise language that conveys your message without ambiguity. When in doubt, err on the side of formality—you can always adjust your tone as your relationship with the recipient develops.

Follow-up Strategies

Following up is where the fine line between persistence and pestering is drawn. Your strategy should be determined by the nature of your request and your relationship with the recipient. A good rule of thumb is to wait at least 48 hours before sending a gentle reminder. When you do follow up, add value by including additional information, a different perspective, or an offer to assist further. This not only keeps your request at the top of their inbox but also demonstrates your commitment to the matter at hand.

Interactive Element: Email Checklist Before hitting send, run through this quick checklist to ensure your message is primed for a response:

- Is the subject line clear and compelling?
- Have I stated the email's purpose in the opening line?
- Is the message concise, yet informative?
- Have I used bullet points or short paragraphs for easy reading?
- Does the email include a direct call to action?
- Have I proofread for spelling and grammatical errors?
- Is the tone appropriate and professional?

Visual Element: Infographic on Crafting Effective Emails This infographic illustrates the key components of an effective email, from the subject line to the signature. It provides visual cues on structuring your message

EFFECTIVE COMMUNICATION SKILLS

for maximum impact and includes tips on tone, timing, and follow-up strategies.

In today's fast-paced digital world, mastering the art of email communication is indispensable. By focusing on conciseness, clarity, compelling subject lines, professional tone, and strategic follow-ups, your emails will not only stand out in crowded inboxes but will also foster stronger, more productive professional relationships. Remember, in digital correspondence, every word counts, and every email is an opportunity to make a lasting impression.

The Dos and Don'ts of Text Messaging in Business

In the digital tapestry of modern business communication, text messaging emerges as a double-edged sword. On one edge, its immediacy and brevity offer unparalleled convenience; on the other, its casual nature harbors the potential for misinterpretation. This section navigates the intricate balance between leveraging text messaging for its efficiency while maintaining the decorum expected in professional interactions.

Appropriateness of Texting

The decision to use text messaging as a business communication tool should not be taken lightly. Its appropriateness hinges on several factors, including the nature of the message, the relationship with the recipient, and the established norms within your industry or organization. As a rule, texts are well-suited for quick updates, scheduling confirmations, and brief queries. However, they fall short for complex discussions, sensitive information, or anything that warrants a detailed response. Always gauge the recipient's openness to texting in a business context, and when in doubt, default to more formal channels.

Brevity vs. Information

Striking a balance between keeping messages brief and conveying necessary information is the crux of effective business texting. The goal is to respect the recipient's time without sacrificing clarity. Begin with a greeting that acknowledges the recipient, followed by a concise statement of your purpose. If the message requires action, be explicit about what is needed and by when. Should the complexity of the topic exceed what can be reasonably communicated in a few lines, suggest a follow-up via email or a call.

- Start with a polite acknowledgment: "Good morning, [Name],"
- Clearly state the purpose: "Wanted to confirm our meeting time tomorrow,"
- Specify any action needed: "Could you please send over the report by the end of today?"
- Offer an alternative for more complex discussions: "Can we schedule a call to discuss further?"

Managing Expectations

Clear communication about when and how text messaging will be used sets the foundation for effective digital interactions. Establish early on what types of messages are appropriate for texting and during what hours. This clarity not only prevents potential oversteps but also aligns expectations, ensuring that urgency and importance are communicated effectively. For instance, specifying that texts should only be sent for matters requiring immediate attention helps to distinguish them from emails or other forms of communication that can be addressed in due course.

Texting Etiquette

The informal nature of texting tempts a departure from the professionalism that guides other business communications. To navigate this, a set of etiquette guidelines can ensure that professionalism remains intact:

- Use of Language: While brevity is key, avoid overly casual language, slang, or abbreviations that might not be universally understood. Stick to clear, straightforward language that leaves little room for misinterpretation.
- Emojis and Shorthand: The use of emojis or shorthand (e.g., LOL, BRB) should be approached with caution. Though they

can imbue a touch of personality or clarity to messages, their appropriateness varies widely depending on your relationship with the recipient and the company culture. When in doubt, leave them out.

- Punctuation and Capitalization: A message entirely in lowercase or lacking punctuation can come across as rushed or unprofessional. Similarly, excessive capitalization may be interpreted as shouting.

- Response Time: Be mindful of the expectation for a quick response that text messaging inherently carries. If a prompt reply isn't feasible, acknowledge the message with a brief note indicating when you will be able to respond in full.

- Privacy and Discretion: Remember that texts are easily forwarded or accessed. Avoid sharing sensitive or confidential information via text. If a topic requires discretion, opt for a more secure communication channel.

Interactive Element: Quiz on Text Messaging Scenarios Test your understanding of business texting etiquette with a quiz that presents various scenarios, asking you to choose the most appropriate way to handle each via text message. This interactive element provides immediate feedback, reinforcing best practices and highlighting common pitfalls to avoid.

In the rapidly evolving landscape of business communication, text messaging stands out for its immediacy and convenience. However, its informal nature demands a careful approach to ensure that professionalism is maintained. By adhering to these mentioned guidelines, you can integrate text messaging into your communication toolkit effectively, leveraging its benefits while sidestepping potential drawbacks. Remember, in the digital age, every message—no matter how brief—contributes to your professional image and the relationships you build within the business community.

Leveraging Social Media for Professional Communication

Social media has irrevocably changed the professional communication landscape, transforming it into a dynamic, interactive sphere that transcends traditional boundaries. This shift necessitates a strategic approach to harnessing social media and it's potential as a powerful tool for networking, brand building, and engaging in meaningful dialogue with audiences worldwide.

Choosing the Right Platforms

The plethora of social media platforms available today offers a diverse range of communication styles and audience demographics. Identifying the most suitable platforms for your business communication needs entails evaluating the unique features and user bases of each.

- LinkedIn stands as the colossus of professional networking, ideal for sharing industry insights, career achievements, and engaging with professionals across various sectors.

- Twitter offers immediacy, making it perfect for sharing news, participating in industry conversations, and engaging with audiences through concise, impactful messages.

- Instagram and Pinterest thrive on visual content, allowing businesses to showcase products, company culture, and visually driven stories to engage creatively with their audience.

- Facebook provides a versatile space for creating community-driven interactions through pages, groups, and detailed post content.

Navigating these platforms effectively requires a clear understanding of your communication goals and the preferences of your target audience. Tailoring your social media presence to platforms that align with your objectives and audience interests ensures your efforts resonate more profoundly and deliver greater impact.

Content Strategy for Engagement

Engaging content forms the backbone of successful social media communication. Crafting content that sparks dialogue, conveys your brand's voice, and builds professional relationships involves a mix of creativity, strategic planning, and responsiveness.

- Value-driven content that addresses your audience's needs, questions, and interests fosters engagement and positions your brand as a thought leader in your industry.

- Interactive content, including quizzes, polls and Q&A sessions, invites participation and feedback, creating a two-way dialogue that enriches the user experience.

- Storytelling through posts, videos, and live sessions can humanize your brand, share your journey, and connect on a more personal level with your audience.

- Consistency and variety in posting schedules and content types maintain audience interest and engagement over time, keeping your brand top-of-mind.

Developing a content calendar, leveraging analytics to understand what resonates with your audience, and staying attuned to trends and conversations within your industry can refine your strategy for maximum engagement.

Personal vs. Professional Presence

The convergence of personal and professional lives on social media necessitates careful management of your online persona. The decision to separate or integrate your personal and professional presence should be guided by your industry, professional goals, and personal comfort with sharing.

- Separation involves maintaining distinct profiles for personal and professional use, allowing you to tailor content and interactions to each audience without crossover.

- Integration requires a balanced approach, where personal insights and professional content coexist, offering a holistic view of your persona. This approach can enhance relatability and trust but demands careful curation to maintain professionalism.

Whichever strategy you choose, transparency, authenticity, and respect for privacy and boundaries remain paramount. These principles ensure that your social media presence reflects your professional ethos and fosters genuine connections.

Crisis Management

In the fast-paced realm of social media, communication crises can emerge with startling speed, posing significant challenges to brand reputation. Effective crisis management on social media hinges on preparedness, transparency, and swift, thoughtful action.

- Preparation involves having a crisis communication plan that outlines potential scenarios, response strategies, and key messaging to ensure a coordinated and efficient response.

- Monitoring social media channels for mentions, sentiment, and emerging issues allows you to identify and address crises early before they escalate.

- Transparency and accountability in your responses help to rebuild trust and demonstrate your commitment to rectifying the situation. Acknowledge the issue, apologize if necessary, and outline steps being taken to resolve it.

- Post-crisis evaluation and learning are crucial. Analysing the crisis-handling process, audience reactions and the impact on your brand provides valuable insights for strengthening your crisis management strategy for the future.

Navigating social media for professional communication demands a nuanced understanding of the platforms, a strategic approach to content creation, careful management of your online persona, and readiness to address crises with grace and responsibility. By embracing these principles, you can unlock the full potential of social media, transforming it into a vibrant channel for meaningful professional interactions, brand building, and audience engagement.

Video Conferencing: Tips for Effective Virtual Meetings

The digital revolution has seamlessly integrated video conferencing into our daily professional routines, transforming our approach to remote communication. This evolution requires a meticulous setup, engaging delivery, and a keen understanding of privacy and technical troubleshooting to ensure productive and effective virtual meetings.

EFFECTIVE COMMUNICATION SKILLS

Preparation and Setup

A successful video conference begins long before the meeting starts, with attention to both technical setup and personal presentation.

- Technical Essentials: Verify your internet connection's stability and speed to avoid disruptions. Use a reliable video conferencing platform familiar to all participants. Test your microphone, speakers, and webcam to ensure they're functioning optimally. Consider using a headset for clearer audio.

- Visual Presentation: Position your camera at eye level to simulate a face-to-face conversation. Good lighting is crucial; natural light is preferable, but if that's not possible, ensure your face is well-lit without harsh shadows. Choose a background that is professional and free of distractions. A tidy, neutral background or a subtle virtual backdrop can minimize distractions and maintain focus on you.

- Personal Readiness: Dress as you would for an in-person business meeting. This not only affects how others perceive you but also how you feel and perform. Review the meeting agenda in advance and have any necessary documents or notes ready for reference.

Engagement Strategies

Maintaining engagement in a virtual setting challenges even the most experienced professionals. Implementing interactive elements and fostering an inclusive environment can keep participants focused and contribute actively.

- Active Participation: Encourage everyone to turn on their cameras, creating a more personal and engaging meeting atmosphere. Begin with a brief roundtable, allowing each participant to introduce themselves or provide updates, fostering a sense of involvement.

- Use of Interactive Tools: Many video conferencing platforms offer tools like polls, whiteboards, and breakout rooms. Utilize these features to break monotony, solicit input, and encourage collaboration.

- Regular Check-Ins: Periodically pause to solicit questions or comments. This ensures that participants remain engaged and provides opportunities to clarify or dive deeper into discussion points.

- Dynamic Delivery: Vary your tone and pace to keep the presentation lively. If you're sharing your screen, use a pointer or highlighter tool to guide attention. Short, periodic breaks during longer meetings can prevent fatigue and maintain focus.

Recording and Privacy

The ability to record video meetings is a valuable feature for documentation and for those unable to attend live. However, it raises important considerations around consent and privacy.

- Consent Is Key: Always inform participants before recording. Provide clear information on how the recording will be used and stored. In some jurisdictions, recording without consent can have legal implications.

- Disclosure of Recording: At the start of the meeting, verbally notify participants that the session will be recorded and reiterate the purpose. This transparency fosters trust and allows participants to adjust their participation if they have privacy concerns.

- Secure Storage: Store recordings securely and limit access to those who need it. Be mindful of sensitive information discussed during the meeting and consider editing or omitting parts of the recording if necessary.

Overcoming Technical Issues

Despite the best preparations, technical glitches can and do occur. Being equipped to address them promptly minimizes disruptions.

- Immediate Troubleshooting: Familiarize yourself with common issues and quick fixes, such as adjusting audio settings or reconnecting to the meeting. Having a technical support contact on standby can be invaluable for more complex problems.

- Plan B: Always have a backup plan. This could be switching to an audio-only call if the video fails or moving to a different platform if the original one malfunctions.

- Post-Meeting Follow-Up: If significant technical issues disrupted the meeting, consider sending a summary or recording to all members. This ensures that everyone is aligned and has access to the discussed information.

In an era where virtual meetings bridge the gap between distant teams, mastering the intricacies of video conferencing is indispensable for professionals. From the initial setup to fostering engagement and navigating privacy and technical challenges, each element plays a pivotal role in conducting successful and productive meetings. By adhering to these guidelines, professionals can leverage the full potential of virtual meetings, ensuring clear, effective, and inclusive communication across digital platforms.

Managing Digital Distractions: Maintaining Focus in a Connected World

In today's hyper-connected environment, digital distractions are an ever-present challenge, subtly eroding our concentration and diminishing our capacity for deep work. This segment explores methods to identify these distractions, strategies to minimize their impact, and approaches to crafting spaces that foster focus and productivity.

Identifying Distractions

The first step in combating digital distractions is to recognize their sources. Common culprits include incessant email notifications, the allure of social media, and the convenience of web browsing. These distractions fragment our attention, making it difficult to engage in focused, meaningful work. To pinpoint your primary digital distractions, keep a log for a week, noting each time you find your attention diverted from a task. This exercise can reveal patterns in your distraction habits and the specific digital tools that disrupt your focus most frequently.

Strategies for Minimizing Distractions

Once identified, several strategies can be employed to mitigate the impact of these digital interruptions:

- **App Blockers:** Use applications designed to limit access to distracting websites or apps during work hours. Tools like Cold Turkey or Freedom allow you to specify which sites to block and when, helping you stay on track.

- **Specific Check-in Times:** Schedule predetermined times to check email and social media, rather than responding to notifications as they arrive. This approach helps consolidate distractions into manageable intervals, freeing up longer periods for focused work.

- **Notification Management:** Take control of your notification settings across devices. Disabling non-essential notifications can significantly reduce interruptions, allowing you to concentrate on the task at hand.

- **The Two-Minute Rule:** For tasks or responses that can be completed in two minutes or less, tackle them immediately. This method prevents small tasks from accumulating and becoming a source of distraction later on.

Creating a Focused Workspace

Designing both physical and digital workspaces that encourage concentration is pivotal. A well-organized desk, free from clutter, sets a tone of order and purpose. Similarly, a digital desktop organized with only essential folders and files minimizes visual clutter and simplifies the retrieval of necessary materials.

- **Dedicated Work Zones:** Establish areas of your workspace for specific activities. Having a place reserved solely for deep work can cue your mind to focus when you're in that space.

- **Ergonomic Considerations:** Comfort plays a crucial role in maintaining focus. Invest in an ergonomic chair and desk setup that minimizes physical discomfort, allowing you to concentrate for longer periods.

- Digital Cleanse: Regularly review and close unnecessary tabs, uninstall unused apps, and declutter your digital files. A streamlined digital environment can reduce cognitive load and aid concentration.

Balancing Connectivity with Productivity

In an era where being constantly connected is often seen as a virtue, striking a balance between accessibility and productivity is essential. This balance requires setting clear boundaries around your availability and communicating these boundaries effectively to colleagues and clients.

- Scheduled Availability: Inform your team of the hours you're focusing on deep work and less available for immediate response. This clarity helps manage expectations and respects your need for uninterrupted work time.

- Email Auto-Responders: Use auto-responders judiciously to notify senders when you're in deep work mode and when they can expect a reply. This tool can alleviate the pressure to respond immediately, allowing you to focus on the task at hand.

- Selective Connectivity: Choose communication tools that align with the nature of your work. For instance, instant messaging may be suitable for quick questions, while email might be better for detailed discussions. Selectively using these tools based on communication needs can optimize your productivity.

In navigating the digital landscape of the modern workplace, identifying distractions, employing strategies to minimize their impact, and creating spaces conducive to focus are key to maintaining productivity. By adopting these practices, you can reclaim your attention and devote it to the work that truly matters, achieving a harmonious balance between the demands of connectivity and the need for deep, meaningful work.

The Art of Digital Listening: Engaging with Your Online Audience

In the expansive realm of the digital world, where every comment, like, and share is a whisper into the void, the skill of digital listening stands as a beacon for those intent on truly understanding and connecting with their audience. This segment is dedicated to unravelling the nuances of digital listening, a critical component in cultivating a meaningful online presence and fostering robust digital relationships.

Principles of Digital Listening

At its core, digital listening transcends mere observation; it's an active process of seeking out and absorbing the myriad voices of your online audience. It's about piecing together the digital murmurs to form a coherent understanding of the public's perception of your brand, their needs, preferences, and pain points. Herein lies the first principle of digital listening: it's not simply about monitoring mentions but about understanding the sentiment and context behind them. The second principle emphasizes responsiveness. Digital listening is not a passive activity; it demands action – be it through engaging with feedback, adapting strategies, or innovating in response to the insights gathered. The final principle underscores the ongoing nature of digital listening. It's a continuous cycle of listening, understanding, acting, and then listening anew.

Tools for Monitoring Online Conversations

To navigate the vastness of the digital landscape, several tools have been designed to aid in the process of digital listening. These range from simple, free tools to sophisticated platforms offering in-depth analytics. Google Alerts serves as a straightforward, no-cost option for monitoring mentions of your brand or relevant keywords across the web. For a more comprehensive solution, platforms like Mention, Brandwatch, and Hootsuite provide real-time tracking across multiple social media channels and websites, along with sentiment analysis to gauge the emotional tone of the mentions. Utilizing these tools allows you to stay attuned to conversations about your brand, industry trends, and competitor activity, offering a panoramic view of your digital ecosystem.

Responding Effectively

The art of response in digital listening is delicate; it requires a balance between timeliness, tone, and transparency. Firstly, timeliness is crucial – the digital world moves quickly, and so should you when responses are required. Whether it's addressing feedback, answering questions, or engaging in conversations, prompt responses signify that you value your audience's input. The tone of your responses should reflect your brand's voice – consistent, respectful, and authentic. It's this authenticity that fosters trust and rapport with your audience. Lastly, transparency in your responses, especially when handling criticism or complaints, demonstrates integrity and a commitment to improvement. Every response is an opportunity to reinforce your brand's values and to turn potential negatives into positives.

Leveraging Insights

The insights gleaned from digital listening are invaluable, wielding the power to transform your communication strategies and business decisions. These insights can help tailor your content strategy to better resonate with your audience, highlighting topics of interest, preferred formats, and optimal posting times. They can also inform product development and innovation by revealing unmet needs or gaps in the market. Furthermore, understanding the sentiment towards your brand can guide reputation management efforts, helping to amplify positive perceptions and address any negative feedback proactively. The key lies in integrating these insights into your planning and decision-making processes, ensuring that your strategies are continuously refined to align with your audience's evolving preferences and expectations.

In the realm of digital communication, where every interaction leaves a trace and every silence speaks volumes, mastering the art of digital listening is imperative. It empowers you to navigate the digital landscape with insight and foresight, to connect with your audience on a deeper level, and to craft strategies that are not just reactive but proactive and informed by a genuine understanding of the digital dialogue surrounding your brand. Through diligent application of digital listening principles, leveraging the right tools for monitoring, responding with care and authenticity, and harnessing insights for strategic advantage, you position yourself not just as a speaker but as a listener – a crucial distinction in the digital age where meaningful engagement is the currency of success.

Building Trust and Rapport Online

In the digital age, where interactions often lack the warmth of a handshake or the immediacy of face-to-face conversation, establishing trust and rapport online becomes a nuanced task. It demands a careful blend of transparency, consistency, personalized interactions, and a showcase of credibility. This section explores how to cultivate these elements to forge deeper connections in the virtual world.

Transparency and Authenticity

In the realm of pixels and screens, where authenticity can sometimes be obscured by the curated nature of digital content, transparency becomes the cornerstone of trust. Being open about your business practices, acknowledging mistakes, and sharing your journey with honesty invites your audience into a transparent relationship.

- **Behind-the-Scenes Glimpses:** Share insights into your work processes, challenges, and successes. This not only humanizes your brand but also demonstrates a willingness to be open with your audience.

- **Honest Communication:** When issues arise, address them directly with your audience. Honesty in difficult times can significantly enhance trust and loyalty.

Consistent Communication

Consistency in your online interactions reinforces reliability. Your audience comes to know what to expect from you, which in turn builds a comfortable familiarity and trustworthiness.

- **Regular Updates:** Maintain a steady rhythm of communication, be it through social media posts, newsletters, or blog updates. This regularity assures your audience of your ongoing presence and engagement.

- **Unified Voice Across Channels:** Ensure your communication tone and style are consistent across all digital platforms. A cohesive voice strengthens your brand identity and fosters trust.

Personalized Interactions

In a digital environment that can sometimes feel impersonal, tailoring interactions to the individual can significantly elevate the sense of connection and rapport with your audience.

- Addressing Individuals: When responding to comments or messages, address the person by name. This small gesture can transform a generic interaction into a personal exchange, making the individual feel valued and seen.

- Segmentation in Email Marketing: Use segmentation tools to customise your email campaigns to match the specific interests and needs of varying segments of your audience. Personalized content resonates more deeply and reinforces the feeling of a one-on-one relationship.

Showcasing Credibility

In the vast sea of online content, establishing your authority and credibility sets you apart, underpinning the trust your audience places in you.

- Sharing Expertise: Regularly contribute valuable content that showcases your knowledge and expertise in your field. This could be through informative blog posts, insightful webinars, or engaging how-to videos.

- Leveraging Testimonials and Reviews: Positive feedback from satisfied customers or clients serves as a powerful endorsement of your credibility. Feature these testimonials prominently on your website and social media channels.

- Engaging with Industry Leaders: Collaborate with respected figures in your field on projects or content. Their endorsement can lend significant credibility to your brand.

Building trust and rapport online requires a concerted effort to be transparent, consistently engage with your audience, personalize interactions, and demonstrate your credibility. These efforts lay the foundation for a robust online presence characterized by deep connections and mutual respect. By prioritizing these principles, you create an environment where trust thrives, paving the way for lasting relationships in the digital domain.

Digital Body Language: Understanding the New Cues

In the tapestry of digital communication, nonverbal cues evolved into what we now recognize as digital body language. This new realm of expression transcends the physical, manifesting in our online behaviours, response times, and even the structure of our messages. Grasping the subtleties of digital body language enables us to navigate online interactions with greater nuance and understanding.

Interpreting Digital Cues

Digital body language encompasses a variety of signals that, while less tangible than traditional nonverbal cues, are equally telling. Consider the length of the messages you receive; a brief, to-the-point email may signal efficiency or, in some contexts, a lack of interest. Conversely, a detailed, thoughtfully crafted message often indicates a higher level of engagement and investment in the conversation. Similarly, the choice of words plays a pivotal role. The use of formal language versus casual, colloquial expressions can reflect the sender's comfort level and relationship with the recipient. Recognizing these cues demands an attentiveness to the digital nuances that colour our online exchanges.

- Message Length: Short, concise messages versus long, detailed correspondences can indicate the sender's engagement level and intent.

- Word Choice: Formal language may show professionalism or distance, while casual wording suggests familiarity and comfort.

The Significance of Response Times

Few aspects of digital body language are as impactful as the timing of responses. A prompt reply can communicate eagerness and interest, while delayed responses may be interpreted as disinterest or neglect. However, this is not a one-size-fits-all rule. The expected response time often depends on the established norms within a particular relationship or organization, as well as the communication channel being used. An immediate reply might be anticipated in instant messaging platforms, whereas email may allow for a more extended timeframe. Sensitivity to these expectations is crucial, as misunderstanding the implied message behind response times can lead to misinterpretation of the sender's intent or level of interest.

- Instant Messaging: Typically expects quicker responses, signalling attentiveness and priority.
- Email: Allows for longer response times, with the understanding that replies may be more considered and detailed.

Tone in Written Communication

Tone breathes life into written communication, infusing it with emotion and intent that the words alone may not convey. In digital interactions, where the absence of vocal inflection and physical presence strips communication to its bare essence, the tone becomes the soul of the message. It is crafted through the choice of words, punctuation, and even the rhythm of the sentences. A well-placed exclamation mark can convey enthusiasm, while a carefully worded question can soften a request, making it more palatable. Striking the right tone requires an alignment with the context of the conversation and an understanding of the relationship between the parties involved. It is a delicate balance that can significantly enhance the clarity and impact of digital exchanges.

- Punctuation: Utilizing exclamation marks for enthusiasm, periods for statements, and ellipses for pauses or continuation.
- Sentence Structure: Short, straightforward sentences can convey clarity and decisiveness, while longer, more complex sentences suggest thoroughness and consideration.

Visual Cues in Video Calls

As video conferencing becomes a staple in professional communication, understanding and utilizing visual cues during these calls is paramount. The positioning of the camera, for instance, can influence the perceived level of engagement; a camera placed too low might give the impression of looking down on others, while eye-level placement fosters a sense of equality. Similarly, maintaining eye contact with the camera, as opposed to looking at the screen, can mimic the eye contact made during in-person interactions, strengthening the connection with the audience. Additionally, nodding or leaning in slightly can convey interest and agreement, mirroring the affirming gestures used in face-to-face conversations. Mastering these visual cues can significantly enhance the effectiveness and personal connection in video communications.

- Camera Positioning: Adjusting the camera to eye level to simulate direct eye contact and foster a sense of engagement.

- Eye Contact: Looking directly at the camera to mimic in-person eye contact, enhancing the sense of connection.

- Nodding and Leaning In: Using nods and slight leans to show agreement, understanding, or interest, akin to physical cues in direct interactions.

In this era where digital interactions predominate, understanding the language of digital body language is indispensable. By mastering the interpretation and conveyance of digital cues, we not only enhance our ability to communicate effectively online but also deepen our connections in a world where physical cues are often absent. As we navigate this digital landscape, let us remain attuned to the subtle signals that enrich our communications, bridging the gap between the physical and the digital, and fostering relationships that thrive in both realms.

Crafting Your Digital Persona: Consistency Across Platforms

In today's digital landscape, where every tweet, post, and email contributes to how you are perceived, the creation of a cohesive digital persona has never been more vital. This persona acts as your virtual handshake, offering a first and lasting impression that spans across the myriad of platforms available at our fingertips. To navigate this process, a deep dive into the elements that sculpt a digital persona aligned with professional aspirations and brand identity is essential.

Defining Your Digital Persona

Before you can project a consistent identity across the digital realm, you must first crystallize what that identity is. Begin by reflecting on your core values, the aspects of your professional life you're eager to highlight, and the goals you aim to achieve through your online presence. Consider your digital persona as your brand's ambassador - it should authentically represent who you are, what you stand for, and where you see yourself in the landscape of your industry. Crafting this persona requires a thoughtful amalgamation of your professional achievements, your unique insights and perspectives, and the tone and style that naturally represent you.

- Identify the attributes you want to be known for, such as reliability, creativity, or expertise in a specific area.

- Determine the aspects of your personal story that you're comfortable sharing and that add depth to your professional narrative.

- Decide on a tone and voice that feel authentic to you, whether that's approachable and conversational or more formal and authoritative.

Consistency Across Platforms

Once your digital persona is defined, the next step is to ensure that it is consistently represented across all digital platforms. This consistency is crucial in building recognition and trust with your audience. It encompasses everything from the visual elements, such as profile pictures and colour schemes, to the verbal, including your messaging and the way you engage with others online.

- Use the same profile picture across platforms to aid in recognition.

- Align your bio or profile description across networks, adjusting only as necessary to fit the platform's tone.

- Ensure that your content themes and areas of expertise are clearly reflected in what you share and discuss across different channels.

Maintaining this consistency helps your audience to quickly recognize and connect with you, no matter where they encounter your digital presence.

Adapting Without Losing Identity

While consistency is key, so too is the ability to adapt your communication style to suit the nuances of different platforms without diluting your core identity. LinkedIn demands a more professional tone and content focused on industry insights, whereas Instagram allows for a more personal glimpse into your professional life through images and stories. The challenge lies in navigating these adjustments without compromising the authenticity of your digital persona.

- For professional platforms like LinkedIn, focus on sharing industry-related content, insights, and professional updates that reinforce your expertise.

- On more visual and personal platforms, such as Instagram, tie personal stories or experiences back to your professional themes, showing the person behind the profession.

- In more casual settings like Twitter, you can adopt a lighter tone but remain mindful to keep conversations and content aligned with your professional goals and persona.

These adaptations allow you to engage effectively across the spectrum of digital platforms, reaching a broader audience while staying true to your defined persona.

Evaluating and Adjusting Your Persona

The digital world is in constant flux, with new trends emerging and audience preferences evolving. As such, your digital persona should not be static. Regular evaluation and refinement ensure that your online identity remains relevant, engaging, and aligned with your evolving professional journey.

- Schedule periodic reviews of your digital presence, assessing whether each element of your persona still accurately reflects your current professional status and goals.

- Solicit feedback from trusted peers or mentors on your digital presence. External perspectives can offer invaluable insights into how you are perceived online.

- Stay attuned to changes in digital communication trends and platform dynamics, adjusting your strategies to maintain effectiveness and engagement.

This ongoing process of evaluation and adjustment allows your digital persona to grow and evolve alongside your professional journey, ensuring it remains a true and dynamic reflection of your brand and identity in the digital world.

The Future of Communication: Trends to Watch

In the evolving landscape of digital communication, staying abreast of emerging trends and technologies is not just advantageous; it is pivotal for anyone looking to maintain relevance and effectiveness in their interactions. This section peels back the curtain on the advancements that are set to redefine the way we connect, share, and engage in the digital realm.

Emerging Digital Communication Tools

The digital toolbox for communication is expanding rapidly, introducing innovative platforms and tools designed to enhance connectivity and engagement. Virtual reality (VR) and augmented reality (AR) are at the forefront, offering immersive experiences that could revolutionize customer engagement, team collaboration, and training methodologies. Imagine conducting a team meeting in a virtual workspace that simulates your office environment or exploring a product prototype in 3D space from anywhere in the world. Similarly, blockchain technology promises to introduce new levels of security and transparency in communication, particularly in contractual and financial exchanges. These tools not only promise to improve the way we communicate but also how we experience and perceive digital interactions.

- Virtual and Augmented Reality: Transforming engagement through immersive experiences.
- Blockchain: Enhancing security and transparency in digital transactions.

The Role of AI in Communication

Artificial Intelligence (AI) is swiftly emerging as a cornerstone in the automation and enhancement of digital communication. AI-driven chatbots and virtual assistants are already commonplace, offering customer support and engagement across various digital platforms. Beyond these applications, AI is set to personalize communication further, analysing user data to tailor messages and content dynamically to the individual's preferences and behaviours. This level of personalization aims to deepen engagement and connection, making digital interactions more relevant and meaningful to each user.

- AI-driven Personalization: Tailoring communication to individual preferences and behaviours for deeper engagement.

Privacy and Security Considerations

As digital communication technologies advance, so too does the complexity of privacy and security concerns associated with them. The integration of AI and blockchain in communication tools offers promising solutions for enhancing data security and user privacy. Encrypted messaging apps, secure data transactions, and anonymized user interactions are just the beginning. However, these technologies also require a nuanced understanding of ethical considerations, regulatory compliance, and the potential for misuse. Vigilance and proactive measures are essential to ensure that advancements in communication technology do not come at the expense of user trust and safety.

- Enhanced Security Measures: Leveraging AI and blockchain for secure and private digital interactions.

- Ethical and Regulatory Compliance: Navigating the complexities of privacy laws and ethical considerations in the use of advanced communication technologies.

Adapting to Changing Communication Landscapes

The only constant in the digital world is change. Adjusting to the changing landscape of digital communication requires a mindset of continuous learning and flexibility. It involves staying informed about technological advancements, understanding the implications of these changes, and being willing to experiment with new tools and platforms.

Equally important is the need to foster digital literacy within teams and organizations, ensuring that all members are equipped to navigate and leverage the benefits of new communication technologies effectively.

- Continuous Learning: Staying informed and adaptable to leverage emerging communication tools.
- Fostering Digital Literacy: Equipping teams with the knowledge and skills to utilize advanced communication technologies.

In closing, the horizon of digital communication is broadening with each technological advancement, bringing with it new tools, challenges, and opportunities. From the immersive experiences offered by VR and AR to the personalized engagement driven by AI, the future promises a landscape where digital interactions are more secure, engaging, and tailored than ever before. Yet, as we venture into this future, the importance of navigating these advancements with an eye toward privacy, security, and ethical considerations remains paramount. In doing so, we not only enhance our ability to communicate but also ensure that these advancements serve to deepen, rather than diminish, our connections with others.

As we turn the page, our exploration continues, delving into the practical applications of these emerging trends and how they can be integrated into our digital communication strategies. The journey ahead is one of discovery, innovation, and adaptation, promising to reshape the fabric of our digital interactions in ways we are only beginning to imagine.

You Are Awesome!

Hey there, amazing reader!

Have you ever thought about the magic of sharing your thoughts? How can a few words from you spark a change, help someone decide, or even transform a life or career? That's the power you hold when you leave a review. It's not just about giving feedback. It's about creating ripples of positivity and knowledge. And guess what? Your insights on "Effective Communication Skills" could be the one thing that guides others towards their path of improvement.

Now, I've got a little brain tickler for you. When was the last time someone's advice or a tip made your day, or better yet, made something click for you? It felt good, right? Imagine being that lightbulb moment for someone else. By sharing your takeaways from the book, you become part of someone's journey towards better communication, relationships, and career success. It's like passing on a secret recipe for success, and who doesn't love doing that?

Here's the thing, every book is a universe of knowledge, but navigating this cosmos can be tricky without the star map of reviews. Your review is that star map guiding other entrepreneurs and business owners to the treasures within. It's about connecting, sharing, and helping others discover the strategies that can change the game for them, just as they did for you.

So, here comes the 'big ask. Would you mind sharing your thoughts on the book? An honest, from-the-heart review on Amazon can light the way for others. Whether it's a strategy that resonated with you, a chapter that changed your perspective, or how this book has impacted your relationships and career growth, your insights are invaluable.

Leaving a review is a breeze:

EFFECTIVE COMMUNICATION SKILLS

- Head to where you got the book
- Search for my book by title or author name and click on its page
- Scroll to "Write a Review" or similar button
- Rate my book with hopefully 5 stars (wink)
- Share your thoughts, experiences, and how the book has influenced your communication skills
- Hit the submit button to share your review

Your review is more than just feedback. It's the words that can positively impact others' lives. It's about passing on the torch of knowledge and helping the community grow stronger, one review at a time.

And hey, in the spirit of sharing and goodwill, think of your review as your way of introducing something invaluable to someone's life. It's about contributing to a circle of growth, understanding, and mutual support. Your words could be the very nudge someone needs to start on their journey of self-improvement and career advancement.

So, are you ready to make a difference with a few words? Your review isn't just appreciated; it's a vital piece of the puzzle for creating a world of better communicators and listeners. Let's spread the word and help others unlock the power of effective communication. Thank you, you awesome communicator!

Conclusion

In the chapters that have unfolded, I have endeavoured to illuminate the transformative power of communication—a journey through the intricacies of active listening, the subtleties of nonverbal cues, the nuances of digital interaction, and the profound psychological underpinnings that govern our exchanges. This odyssey from the foundational stones of effective communication to the sophisticated application of these principles in the pulsating digital age underscores the expansive and comprehensive nature of the learning journey we have embarked upon together.

Reflecting on this journey, it is evident that the mastery of communication skills extends far beyond mere transactional interactions; it is the cornerstone of building enduring personal relationships and achieving unprecedented business success. Through practical strategies, engaging exercises, and real-world examples, this book has armed you with an arsenal of tools poised for immediate application, aiming to elevate your communication prowess to new heights.

As we draw this exploration to a close, I invite you to pause and reflect on your current communication habits. Identify areas ripe for application and growth based on the insights gleaned from these pages. Which aspects of your communication style hold the potential for transformation? Where can you implement the strategies discussed to forge deeper connections and clearer understanding in your interactions?

I urge you, as your next step, to commit to one actionable strategy that resonates with you. Whether it be honing your active listening skills in your upcoming conversations, recalibrating your digital communication style, or practicing the delicate art of interpreting nonverbal cues—choose a tactic that you can implement immediately. This commitment marks the beginning of your journey toward becoming a more effective communicator, a journey that promises rich rewards in both your personal and professional realms.

View communication as a dynamic skill set, one that thrives on ongoing attention, practice, and adaptation. Cultivate habits around the strategies we have discussed, and remain ever-vigilant for opportunities to expand your repertoire. Seek out further resources, join workshops, attend seminars, and engage with a community of like-minded individuals dedicated to the art of communication. This engagement not only enriches your learning experience but also fosters a sense of community among those of us on this path to improvement.

Remember, the art of communication is not a destination but a journey—one that unfolds with each word spoken, each gesture made, and each message conveyed. As you continue on this path, know that you possess the power to transform your relationships, elevate your career, and catalyse personal growth through the deliberate and skilful practice of communication.

Let this book not be the end but the beginning of an ongoing exploration into the profound impact effective communication can have on your life. Embrace the journey, for in your hands lies the ability to reshape your future, one conversation at a time.

References

- *The Power Of Empathy For Business Growth*
  https://www.forbes.com/sites/forbesbusinesscouncil/2022/03/22/the-power-of-empathy-for-business-growth/

- *Psychological Barriers in Communication (The Silent Challenge)*
  https://barriersofcommunication.com/psychological-barriers-in-communication/

- *7 Active Listening Techniques for Business Development*
  https://www.thebdschool.com/blog/active-listening-techniques#:~:text=Paraphrasing%2C%20reflecting%20feelings%2C%20open%2Dended%20questions%2C%20summarizing%2C%20paying%20attention%20to%20body%20language%2C%20taking%20notes%2C%20and%20avoiding%20distractions%20are%20seven%20active%20listening%20techniques%20that%20can%20help%20business%20development%20professionals%20to%20enhance%20their%20communication%20skills.

- *Using Body Language in Negotiation - PON*
  https://www.pon.harvard.edu/daily/negotiation-skills-daily/negotiation-techniques-and-body-language-body-language-negotiation-examples-in-real-life/

- *Storytelling That Moves People*
  https://hbr.org/2003/06/storytelling-that-moves-people

- *Dr. Robert Cialdini's Seven Principles of Persuasion | IAW*
  https://www.influenceatwork.com/7-principles-of-persuasion/

- *Fear of public speaking: How can I overcome it? - Mayo Clinic*
  https://www.mayoclinic.org/diseases-conditions/specific-phobias/expert-answers/fear-of-public-speaking/faq-20058416

- *How To Create the Perfect Elevator Pitch in 6 Steps - Indeed*
  https://www.indeed.com/career-advice/career-development/perfect-elevator-pitch

- *Negotiation Skills for Win-Win Negotiations - PON*
  https://www.pon.harvard.edu/daily/negotiation-skills-daily/listening-skills-for-maximum-success/

- *Nonverbal Communication and Body Language - HelpGuide.org*
  https://www.helpguide.org/articles/relationships-communication/nonverbal-communication.htm

- *The Power of Listening in Helping People Change*
  https://hbr.org/2018/05/the-power-of-listening-in-helping-people-change

- *Using Body Language in Negotiation - PON*
  https://www.pon.harvard.edu/daily/negotiation-skills-daily/negotiation-techniques-and-body-language-body-language-negotiation-examples-in-real-life/

- *The Power of Eye Contact: Building Trust and Connection*
  https://www.linkedin.com/pulse/power-eye-contact-building-trust-connection-hingston-lovell-dohwc

- *The Importance of Cross-Cultural Communication in Business*
  https://online.yu.edu/syms/blog/global-business-and-cross-cultural-communication

- *10 Tips to Improve Nonverbal Communication*
  https://fellow.app/blog/management/tips-to-improve-nonverbal-communication-in-virtual-meetings/

- *Writing Effective Emails - Getting People to Read and Act ...*
  https://www.mindtools.com/apz815y/writing-effective-emails

- *SMS Texting Etiquette: 14 Tips for Modern Professionals*
  https://www.openphone.com/blog/business-texting-etiquette-tips/

- *Leveraging Social Media in Your Marketing Strategy*
  https://www.wrike.com/blog/leveraging-social-media-marketing/

- *Best Practices For Virtual Presentations: 15 Expert Tips ...* https://www.forbes.com/sites/maryabbajay/2020/04/20/best-practices-for-virtual-presentations-15-expert-tips-that-work-for-everyone/

www.ingramcontent.com/pod-product-compliance
Lightning Source LLC
Chambersburg PA
CBHW072209070526
44585CB00015B/1254